Legends from Ireland

'For Séamus Ó Catháin'

Legends from Ireland

SEAN O'SULLIVAN
Drawings by John Skelton

B. T. BATSFORD LTD
LONDON

First published 1977

© Sean O'Sullivan 1977

ISBN (Cased) 0 7134 0733 6
ISBN (Limp) 0 7134 0734 4

Photoset by Weatherby Woolnough,
Wellingborough, Northants.
Printed by Billings & Son Ltd,
London, Guildford & Worcester

for the Publishers
B. T. BATSFORD LTD
4 Fitzhardinge Street, London W1H 0AH

Contents

IRELAND

Tory Island

Gweedore
Rannafast
Lough Swilly
Aranmore Island
Gartan
Glenveagh
Coleraine

ANTRIM

Derry
DERRY
Ballymena
Bangor
Belfast

DONEGAL
ULSTER
Inver
Donegal Town

Omagh
TYRONE
DOWN
Downpatrick
Lagan

Armagh
Enniskillen
FERMANAGH
Monaghan
ARMAGH
Newry

Sligo
SLIGO
MONAGHAN
Cavan
CAVAN
Magheracloone
LOUTH
Drogheda

MAYO
C O N N A C H T
LEITRIM
Castlebar
Urlar
ROSCOMMON
Longford
LONGFORD
MEATH
Navan
Boyne

Athlone
WESTMEATH
Clontarf
Dublin
GALWAY
Galway
OFFALY
LEINSTER
Tullamore
Liffey
Naas
KILDARE
Bray

Port Laoise
Wicklow
WICKLOW

CLARE
Ennis
LEIX
Carlow
Arklow

Shannon
TIPPERARY
Thurles
Nore
KILKENNY
Kilkenny
CARLOW
Barrow
WEXFORD

Limerick
LIMERICK
Tipperary
Suir
Enniscorthy

M U N S T E R
Tralee
KERRY
Waterford
Wexford

Killarney
CORK
Youghal
WATERFORD
Tramore
Creadan Head
Dungarvan

Lee
Cork
Ballycotton

■ Town or city
○ District
----- County boundary
▬▬▬ Provincial "

0   10   20   30   40 miles

Ⓑ

Foreword

Writing in *The Speaker* when he was twenty-eight years old, Yeats said that: 'Folk-lore is at once the Bible, the Thirty-nine articles, and the Book of Common Prayer, and well-nigh all the great poets have lived by its light. Homer, Aeschylus, Sophocles, Shakespeare, and even Dante, Goethe, and Keats, were little more than folk-lorists with musical tongues.' The overstatement is justified by earlier neglect of the subject, except as a random antiquarian interest. True, by 1893, when Yeats was writing, a change was under way, but it was still long before folklore was recognised as an important repository of human history. Only in recent years has it begun to be accepted as a basic source for the understanding of our intellectual and spiritual background.

From this point of view, Irish legend is unusually valuable. Isolated on what was, for countless centuries, the westernmost fringe of the world, facets of folklore which had disappeared elsewhere were preserved. To this rich harvest must be added the abundance of native Irish lore, fostered by a delight in story-telling.

Yeats, writing at the turn of the century, was giving voice to opinions which, though not expressed in openly radical terms, questioned 19th-century values. Browne, two decades later, mentioned the alien 'politeness' which was stifling traditional Irish society, and against which the Irish cultural revival reacted. During the same period there began, and not only in Ireland, a reassessment of the accepted view of religion, social and political institutions, theories in education, and of the whole bourgeous evaluation of art and culture. Modern folklorists are the beneficiaries of this new outlook, and of the philosophy which Yeats and those like him made intelligible. Recognising the true worth of traditional lore, the wisdom and beauty which it contains, they laid the foundation for a modern reconciliation between the folk arts and the fine arts. The result has been the preservation of much that is vital and entertaining, which otherwise would have been embedded in a lifeless pseudo-romanticism, or lost in fashionable social conformity.

Some sixty years ago, while writing about touring in Ireland, Shaw chided the car-men who took English visitors to see historical sites in the vicinity. A tradition existed among them, so he said, of entertaining the tourists with impersonations of Myles nag Copaleen and Micky Free, characters from early nineteenth-century novels set in Ireland. 'All such performances,' he added, 'are pure humbug and the anecdotes are learned and repeated without sense.' This is very true, but Shaw also used the word tradition, even though he may have chosen it coincidentally. He could therefore have recognised that a tradition is never totally worthless, since it illustrates the society which produces it. In the very changed society of modern Ireland, different traditions have survived or been recorded. This second selection within the present series from the Irish folklore archives, which Sean O'Sullivan so long and ably tended, again shows how fortunate we are that this rich store of folklore has been preserved. How immeasurably poorer we would be if 'traditional' Ireland had been reduced to the caricature of Victorian fictional writers.

John Harrison, discussing Yeats, T. S. Eliot and certain of their contemporaries in a book published a few years ago, pointed out that, in considering the past, they questioned the fashionable view dating back to Marx and Darwin. According to this, the past is insignificant as such, being of interest only in so far as the present grows out of it and it may therefore, to some degree, illuminate current patterns or social trends. This ultra-utilitarianism was, very largely, typical of their era, and it is doubtful whether many serious thinkers would now endorse it. A nation, like an individual, has specific characteristics, and a conscious recognition of all that is genuinely valuable within the national heritage creates a common self-respect, enabling a society to function effectively.

The legends in the present volume are such as will inspire and interest not only Irish readers, but folklorists generally, and especially those in the English-speaking world. Although, to be appreciated by a wider audience, the legends need to be presented in English translation, we should remember that Great Britain – and England itself – owes much to our ancient Celtic background. Of the beautiful old Celtic designs now in use on Irish postage stamps, two originate from within England, a fact stressing that the common heritage is perhaps better recognised in Ireland than in this country. We should be specially grateful, once again, to Sean O'Sullivan for providing such excellent English translations, and for making these splendid legends accessible to us.

London University
January 1977   Venetia Newall

Introduction

From the view-point of the folklorist, Ireland has a strategic geographical position as an island off the west coast of Europe. Much of its lore, at least so far as custom and belief are concerned, derives from that of the Celtic-speaking peoples who once lived in the western lands of that continent. In addition, traces of certain facets of European lore, which have disappeared on the mainland, can still be found in Ireland.

Intensive collection of Irish oral tradition was carried on by the Irish Folklore Commission (1935-1971), and is still being done by the full-time collectors of its successor, the Department of Irish Folklore in University College, Dublin. Indexing of the large body of lore amassed up to now has been going on during the intervening period, but many years will, of necessity, have elapsed before it will be completed.

Hitherto, some representative selections of the material collected have been published, mainly in Irish in journals and books, and the main stress has been on the rich body of folktales which have continued to be told down to our own day. These tales were narrated as a pastime at a time when modern media had not been invented. They have by now served their original purpose and will, in the future, be mainly of interest to academic specialists.

The present volume places a collection of legends before the readers. Since these differ in both nature and origin from folktales, some comment on them may be called for. Folk belief and custom, on which legends are based, reflect the inner mind and behaviour of peoples more closely than do folktales, and they offer a fairly sure key to the ways of thought of our ancestors. The event described in a legend was regarded as an actual happening, so far as the folk – be they rural or townsfolk – were concerned. It might have been an unusual happening which, because of its nature, attracted popular attention and was credible and worthy of being kept alive. In addition to this, a legend was normally local; the places, persons, events and dates mentioned in the story were usually known to both the narrator and the audience. While some legends have wandered far afield, in most cases they are more likely to be associated with some local place or person, if the conditions are suitable. A legend may range from a dimly-remembered event to a detailed account of some more recent unusual experience, often associated with beings from the otherworld – ghosts, fairies, spirits, mermaids and such. At a time when our forefathers believed in the existence of an invisible world close-by, whose inhabitants could, and did, intrude into human affairs for good or ill, the scene was set for innumerable legends which described the contacts.

A legend will die only when its local roots have been severed and popular interest in it has ceased. It thrives best where social change comes slowly, and it is kept alive by constant repetition. As the first telling of a legend is usually more close in time and place to the event which it describes, it is more likely to better preserve the real facts than do later versions when the folk's-eye view dims the outline and fantasy is added to a greater or lesser degree.

In recent years some academics have concentrated on legendry, rather than on folktales, as a subject for serious study. They have found, however, that it is much easier to describe the basic characteristics of a legend than to define what it really is. It is localised; it is factual and often has some historic validity; it is told in ordinary speech, unlike some folktales which have long repetitive 'runs' or rhetorics; it is a straightforward art form and is extremely variable; though usually short, it may, on the lips of an expert narrator, especially when he is telling of a personal experience, reach the length of even a folktale and comprise more than one episode; it describes events which the ordinary man has to face passively; it is credible, so far as the audience is concerned, especially when told in a convincing manner and referring to local persons, places and dates; it does not require a special setting or audience for its narration, as a folktale does, but can be introduced into normal conversation when the topic is relevant; and finally, a legend can have a moral or didactive force when it implies or lays down proper rules of behaviour.

Since legends are based on popular belief, in its many ramifications, it is not surprising that they are to be met with in an astonishing variety in Irish oral tradition. The variants already indexed in Ireland run to hundreds of thousands. Most of them have only a local distribution, but some (like the first legend in the present collection) are to be found in other countries also. These have been named Migratory Legends, some of which have been listed for Norway in a monograph by Professor Reidar Th. Christiansen of Oslo (see Bibliography). Often, however, each legend belongs to the area in which it originated and retains its individuality by its association with particular persons, places and dates.

The present volume contains the first collection of representative legends ever published in Ireland. It offers ninety-three examples in different genres. All are taken from oral tradition and give the personal style of the narrator. Sixteen (Nos. 9, 12, 15, 22, 27, 42, 72, 73, 75, 76a, 77, 81, 83, 87, 88 and 93) are in the English language, just as they were recorded. The remaining seventy-seven are translations which I have made from the original Irish versions, keeping as close as possible to the style of the storytellers. The whole collection, has, therefore, been culled from living oral tradition. No item in it belongs to the 'scissors and paste' variety, which is usually garbled and summarised.

There is no book of this kind in existence. In years gone by, some such volumes were limited in scope (to fairy lore, for example), or else included items which ranged from folktales to translated extracts from early sagas, which were not legends at all. A similar criticism can be applied to some collections of legends published in other countries, which did not offer the individual narratives as examples of real oral tradition.

All of the legends in this volume have been selected by me from the manuscripts in the Department of Irish Folklore in University College, Dublin. They have never before been published in English. The Notes give full references to the original manuscript sources, together with details of the name and address of each narrator and of the collector. Mention is also made in the Notes of those legends from oral tradition, which have been published in Irish, without translation, in *Béaloideas,* the Journal of the Folklore of Ireland Society. I do not claim to have included examples of all available Irish legend-types; this would require several volumes of this size. Both collection and indexing still continue, and it is probable that many new legend-types will be revealed in due course. An all-embracing collection of Irish legends remains for future research-workers and editors.

The segregation of the individual items in this volume, under the different genres, has not been an easy task. Several legends might just as well have been placed in other sections as those in which they appear. For example, stories about the Devil (Section II) might equally well have been placed in Section IV (The Supernatural), and some legends in Section III (Origins) could have been allotted elsewhere. Again, in a country like Ireland, a religious flavour is to be found in many legends which do not, in the main, really belong to Section VI. A choice had to be made, and it is my hope that the Contents, as well as the Motif-Index and the General Index, will serve as a guide through the contents of this volume.

I wish to acknowledge my debt to the various collectors who recorded these stories and to the narrators, many of whom are now dead, who handed them on. I am also grateful to Professor Bo Almqvist, Director of the Irish Folklore Department, for allowing me to use the material, and to the other members of the staff for their assistance.

Seán Ó Súilleabháin

I
Fate

International folktales about Fate and Destiny are listed in Aarne-Thompson, *The Types of the Folktale*, under Types 930-949. They were popular in many countries, not least of all in Ireland.

Legends concerning Fate also occur in Ireland, and four examples follow. As well as these, there are found in Ireland legends of the boy who was fated to drown (and drowns in his own perspiration), and of the man who was fated to be hanged (and underwent the ordeal in a dream-sequence). Some legends of Fate are associated with astrology.

1 *River claims a victim*

At one time there was a man living east there beside Ballaghadoon
Church. One very wet day, he decided to go down the lane towards
the church to cut some spars for thatching his house. He went and
he was cutting the spars. There was a high flood in the river. When
he had been cutting for a good while, he heard a voice over his head
in the air, saying:

'The time has come! But I don't see the person!'

He paid no notice to it. The voice said the same words again, and
said them a third time afterwards. When the voice had spoken the
third time, the man heard the sound of a horse coming down the
lane. He looked up towards it, and saw a man coming riding on a
horse. When the horseman came near, he asked him where was he
going on such a day when the river was so high that he could not
cross over.

'Oh, I must go!' said the horseman.

'Surely you don't have to cross over on a day like this!' said the
man. 'The flood would sweep away every horse in the country, let
alone a man. Come home with me to my house and stay there until
the flood goes down.'

He caught hold of the bridle of the horse and led the horse and
its rider towards his house. They went in, and the horseman sat near
the fire. He wasn't long seated there before he started to fall asleep.
The man of the house told him to throw himself into bed and sleep
for a couple of hours, if he felt like it, and he would wake him in
the evening when the flood had fallen. The horseman went to bed,
and when the people of the house thought that it was time for him
to get up, they went over to the bed and looked in. They wished to
wake him. But the horseman was dead, drowned in a lake of water
on the sheet under his mouth. He was fated to drown. They didn't
know where he had come from. So they sent word around the
country to find out would anybody come to take the horse away.
The horse was running around along the highways, and nobody
knew who owned it or where it had come from, along with its rider.
They never found out anything about the man who was fated to
drown.

For references to a similar type of legend in Norway, see *Folklore
Fellows Communications* (FFC), No. 175 (1958), 'The Migratory

Legends', No. 4050 (River Claiming its Due. 'The hour has come but not the man'); av Klintberg, *Svenska Folksägner,* 79, 291.

In Ireland, the legend is also attached to the River Sulán, near Ballyvourney, County Cork.

2 'The sod of death'

Long ago there was a man living west in Ardnacanny. He was cutting turf over near Binn Diarmada, and he had cut a good deal of it. He sat down to 'redden' his pipe. A voice spoke above his head.

'You are sitting on your sod of death!' said the voice.

The man looked around.

'I'll prove to you that I'm not!' said he.

He cut with his spade the big piece of turf on which he had been sitting. The cliff was close by, and he took the sod along and threw it over the edge. When he went home, he started to tell his wife what had happened and what he had done, saying that it would never come true. A few years later, he was gathering seaweed and he came upon a big lump that had seaweed growing on it.

'By the Devil!' said he. 'If I had you dry near the fire at home, you'd make a nice seat!'

He cut the seaweed off it and took it home. He dried it, and it was put in the corner beside the fire. His wife usually sat on it, until one night she said to him:

'Take the child from me! I have something to do around the house.'

He took the child. He wasn't long seated on the lump when he screamed. The child almost fell from his arms. He died immediately. Then his wife remembered his story. She got a knife and cut the lump to see what kind it was. It was a sod of turf. Didn't it last a long time?

The title of this legend is translated from the usual Irish one, *Fód Báis.* Many versions of it have been recorded in Ireland. For references to the basic legend in early Irish literature, as well as in modern Irish and Swedish oral tradition, see *Arv* 13 (1957), 173-9, 'Fót báis/ banaþúfa', by Maura Carney (Dublin); Strömbäck, *Folklore och Filologi,* 284-95; Holtsmark, *Lochlann* 2 (1962), 'Fód báis-banaþúfa-heillaþúfa'.

3 *Patience overcomes fate*

There used to be poor scholars travelling through Ireland long ago. They would stay maybe a week in a house they liked, or often even a fortnight. But if they didn't like a house or if it didn't suit them very well as lodgings and for good food, they might spend only one night there.

But the story goes that a poor scholar, who was going about at that time, came to a farmer's house. He used to call there whenever he passed that way and might stay for a week or a fortnight. When he came this time a baby boy was born there at night, after he arrived. While the child was being born, the poor scholar went outside. He was able to read the stars or the moon, whichever it was, and find out what was in store for the child until the day of its death.

When he came back into the house, the baby had been born. The poor scholar sat down, wrote a letter, folded it small and gave it to the mother. He told her to cover it with a piece of cloth or leather so that it would stand up to moisture, and the writing would never fade until the child would be able to read it. The child grew up until he went to school. The mother had done as the poor scholar had told her: she covered the letter with a piece of leather or cloth, put a strap on it and hung it about the boy's neck. He had also told her that no one should find out what was in the letter, or ever read it, until the child himself would have learned enough to be able to read it and find out what it said.

One day when the boy was returning from school, fairly strong at the age of ten or twelve years, he was running home in a hurry from school, when this little bundle with the strap rose up from his neck and chest. It was striking against his mouth as he ran, so he took hold of it and tugged at it. It was troubling him, striking him in the mouth and eyes as he ran. He tore off the covering that was on it, and caught sight of the paper and writing. He pulled out the paper, opened it and began to read it.

What was written in the letter was that on a certain day and month and year Fate would kill him. When he reached home, he asked his mother why it was said in the paper that was about his neck as long as he could remember that Fate would kill him. Who had written it and what did it mean at all? His mother told him the whole story about the poor scholar and the letter he wrote the night he was born.

'If that's what's going to happen,' said the mother, 'may God help us! I don't know what we'll do, or how we'll save you.'

When the father came home, he was told about it. He said that he would build a house for the son, with nothing but glass in frames on the outside; nothing could enter except the woman who would attend him and get his food ready. A year went by and the time came when Fate was to kill the young man. He was then twenty-one years of age. The day came when he was to be killed by Fate, according to the letter. He sat on a chair in the little house, at a table, and was reading a book.

He happened to glance out through the glass of the wall and saw a small *piast* (serpent) crawling up along the wooden frame of the glass. When it had reached three or four feet from the ground, it began to make a hole through the frame towards where he sat. It crawled over towards him, but he didn't move. It crawled along his shoe, up along his shin, on to his chest and entered his mouth. The young man never moved a hand to stop it. It came back out of his mouth again and went into each of his nostrils. He never moved. The serpent then went in under one of his eyes, came out and went in under the other eye. It came out again and went into his ears. During all that time, he made no move to stop the serpent. When it had crawled over and entered every part of his body, and he making no move to stop it or drive it away, the serpent went down again to the floor, along his clothes. It then stood up and was changed into a man.

'You are the bravest man in the world!' said he. 'Patience has overcome Fate. You have beaten me. I am Fate. If you had raised a hand against me in any way, while I was crawling over your body, I would have killed you. You are the most patient man in the world today. Therefore, you will have a long life. Fate will never kill you for your Patience has defeated it.'

This type of legend may have been used in medieval and later times as an *exemplum* (moral story used by a preacher during a sermon).

4 *One member of a family fated to die*

Father Foley, the priest who was in the Glen long ago, cured a lot of people. He lived in a thatched house in Ballinahown. Siafra O'Connell was living in Ballinskelligs at that time and he had an only son, who was the equal of a score of men even at the age of twenty. One night a bad sickness came on him, and the doctor was sent for. The doctor said that his life couldn't be saved, with the disease that he had, even if he were the only man in the world. They sent for the priest, Father Foley, to anoint him. When that was done, the boy's mother said to the priest:

'I'd give all I have in the world, Father, if I could save him.'

'I'll do my best,' said the priest.

He drew out his breviary and started to read it aloud. The boy fell asleep, and the priest closed the breviary. When he did so, the boy awoke and was in great pain. The priest opened his breviary again and started to read from it. As he did so, the breviary jumped from his hand.

'Give your son to God,' said he to the boy's mother. 'I have done all in my power for him. I saved the life of his father twenty years ago, but now someone else in the family must go in his stead.'

The boy died that night, and from then on Father Foley never opened his breviary to save the life of anybody.

This legend illustrates the healing and other powers attributed to some priests in Irish oral tradition. The places mentioned are in the barony of Iveragh, in south-west Kerry.

II
The Devil

In a number of folktales, the Devil is not at all the fearsome figure of legends. In the former, he is often outwitted. He is rarely mentioned in the Old Testament, but gained prominence as an evil being in the early centuries of Christianity. In the Middle Ages he assumed grotesque shapes, as an animal with horns, tail and hooves, and in Irish lore often took on human guise. He seems to be a mixture of the biblical adversary, the hoofed Pan or satyr, the demonic *jinn* of the East, and evil spirits in general. In Irish legends, though often overcome or banished, he is to be feared.

5 *The Devil in the guise of the Blessed Virgin*

There were two priests there one time, a parish priest and his coadjutor. The parish priest got a sick-call late one night and, faith, he refused to go. The coadjutor asked him why. He said that it was too late.

'Well,' said the coadjutor, 'as you aren't going, I'll go myself.'

The coadjutor went off on saddle-horse and anointed the dying woman. She died while he was with her. Then he journeyed home, and on the way, he saw three lights coming towards him. One of the lights was very faint as compared to the other two. When they met, he asked the faint light why it was so weak.

'I received only lay baptism, that's why I'm so weak,' said the light.

'If I had anybody now to stand as sponsor in baptism for you, I would stand as your second sponsor and baptise you,' said the priest.

The Virgin Mary appeared at his side.

'I am here,' said she.

The priest baptised the faint light, and when he had done so, it grew as bright as the other two. They were the three dead children of the woman whom he had just anointed before her death. They were now angels in Heaven and had come to meet their dead mother.

'You have done good work tonight,' said the Virgin to the priest, 'better than the parish priest who refused to answer the sick-call. What kept him from answering it was this: he thinks that it is I he sees in his room every night; but it is not I but the Devil, may God save us! for he can appear in human shape.'

The priest made his way home, and the parish priest asked him had he anointed the woman. He said that he had and that she had died.

'I'll go into your room tonight,' said he to the parish priest.

'You won't!' said the parish priest.

'I will!'

'You won't!'

'I will!'

The parish priest had to allow the coadjutor into his room. The two of them were not long there when the Devil came in, in the guise of the Virgin Mary. The coadjutor put on his stole and read a prayer three times. Then he sprinkled the holy water, and the Devil went up the chimney in a flash of flames.

'Now,' said he to the parish priest, 'you see that it was the Devil you had in the guise of the Virgin Mary!'

That's the story.

Children were normally baptised by a priest except when there was imminent danger of death, and lay baptism (*baisteadh urláir:* floor or home baptism) was applied by a non-cleric. In oral tradition, there seems to have been an idea that lay baptism was not as beneficial as Church baptism. The Devil in the guise of a beautiful woman often takes the role of temptress in tales and legends.

6 The Devil as a cat

A young man came out of college, a priest, one time. His father and mother were very well-off. When the priest saw how comfortable they were, he made up his mind to leave home and to travel through the country like any poor person. He would say Mass each Sunday, wherever he might be. So off he went, and travelled along until a day of fog and rain came. Hunger came upon him. He was near a castle, and he said to himself:

'I'll go up to this castle, to see will I get anything to eat.'

The servant-girl saw him approaching and she said to her master:

'There's a Catholic priest coming,' said she. 'What'll I do?'

'Oh, ask him to come in! 'Tis near dinner-time. Invite him in for some dinner!' said her master.

When the priest knocked at the door, the girl invited him to come in.

'My master wants you to have some dinner,' said she.

'Very well,' said the priest.

When he entered, the master of the castle himself was cooking. When he lifted up a chunk of meat, a huge, black cat, that was there, jumped up on a chair. The master cut off the first slice of the meat and gave it to the cat. Then he sliced the rest of the meat, put it on plates, and gave another slice to the cat. When he had given the second slice to the cat, the master and his young family and the priest sat down to eat at the table. The young people went out after they had eaten, and the master of the castle and the priest remained behind to converse.

'What kind of cat is that you have?' asked the priest.

'A wonderful animal! He's the family cat,' said the master.

' 'Tis strange to call him the family cat,' said the priest. 'Why do you say that about him?'

'Well, I think that he belonged to my grandfather, and now he is mine.'

'Any cat that's as old as that will come if you call him,' said the priest.

'Indeed, he will.'

'Call him, until we see!' said the priest.

The master called the cat, but he didn't come.

'Maybe he'll come to you,' said the priest to the servant-girl.

'He never yet ate any bite of food that I cooked,' said the girl. 'Nor would he look at any kind of food I offered him.'

'Oh, wouldn't he?' asked the priest. 'He doesn't have your religion.'

Search was made for the cat, but he wasn't to be found high or low. The priest lit a candle and went up into the attic. There he found the cat sitting in a corner. When the cat saw the candle being brought in, he jumped up, spat on the candle and quenched it.

'I can do without it, but you can't!' said the priest.

'I shouldn't have let you light it,' said the cat.

The priest took the candle downstairs, and he spoke to the servant-girl.

'Bring me some water and salt,' said he.

She brought him the water in some kind of vessel, and the salt. He put on his stole, blessed the water and the candle and went upstairs to the cat again. When the cat saw the light of the candle coming again, he could not bear it. He jumped down to the priest's feet. The priest prayed for a while, and then said to the cat:

'How long have you been here?'

The cat didn't answer. The priest prayed for another while.

'How long have you been here?' he asked.

The cat didn't answer.

'I'm your master now!' said the priest. 'How long have you been here?'

'Since his grandfather's time,' said the cat.

'Where is his grandfather?'

'I have him,' said the cat.

'What are you waiting here for?' asked the priest.

'I'm waiting for himself,' said the cat.

'Well, you won't get him,' said the priest. 'He's too generous a man. Well, the door by which you came in now, that's the door you must leave by.'

He banished the cat out through the wall in a blaze of fire. When the priest was going to leave, the master of the castle was standing by.

'You'll stay here now,' said he to the priest.

'I won't,' said the priest. 'I prefer to suffer hardship rather than stay in a place like this where I'd have plenty to eat and drink. I'll travel on like this until I get a place of my own.'

'If you come around this way again,' said the master of the castle, 'don't come in here. If you do come in, I won't be here. If I turned Catholic now, all here would call me a turncoat! But they won't get a chance of doing that! I will go away to some remote island, where nobody has ever seen me and won't know who I am. I'll become a Catholic. That's why it will be no use for you to come here looking for me, though there may be somebody else here.'

The Devil in the guise of a cat, especially in non-Catholic houses, is often mentioned in folktales and legends. See Kittredge, *Witchcraft,* 37-44, 178; also Thompson, *Types,* No. 217*, 'Devil-cat which Holds Candle'. The suggested conversion of the castle-owner to Catholicism was a usual theme in Irish tales and legends in former times.

7 *Tearless woman cries on seeing the Devil*

There was a young girl there long ago. She became sick so badly that she had to stay in bed and couldn't leave it. Whatever goes on for a long time grows cold, and her people used to leave her alone in the house often and go out working. One day she heard someone coming into the house and asking was there anybody at home. She spoke from the bed and said that she was.

'Could you get up and give me a drink?' asked the stranger.

'I couldn't,' said she. 'I haven't left the bed for a long while.'

He asked her again and again to get up. She felt herself getting a little better than she had felt for a long time, and when she made an effort to get up, she was able to do so. When she went up to the kitchen, where the man was, she saw that she had never laid eyes on him before. She gave him the drink.

'Now,' said he, 'from this on you'll be as well as you ever were. But don't let anything make you sad; if you do, you'll die.'

He went out the door and left her there. 'Tis her people that were delighted when they came home, to find her able to run and jump! From that on, there wasn't a young woman in the townland more sturdy, more strong or more healthy than she. She was a fine, handsome, young woman. She got married a short while after that and, when the time came, she gave birth to a child. The baby died soon after being born. The mother didn't shed a tear over it, as if the child wasn't her own at all. A second child was born after that, and it died in the same way. And so did a third child. She shed no tears for any of them.

That was good and it wasn't bad! An old man who lived near them was dying, and the young woman's mother-in-law said to her:

' 'Tis a shame for us if we don't go to enquire for our neighbour who is dying!'

The pair of them went to spend the night at the old man's house. The old man and Death were struggling with each other. The two women were in the room where he was dying, and towards the end of the night, the young woman gave a terrible scream. She had seen the Devil in the room when the old man was drawing the last breath. The two of them came home in the morning, and they ate a few bites of breakfast as usual. It wasn't long until the mother-in-law said to her son:

'The scream of this woman could be heard far off last night when the old man over there was dying, but a tear didn't come from her eye after her own three children!'

At that moment, the young mother grew sad.

'Go and call the priest!' said she to her husband. 'I haven't long to live!'

The husband did as she asked him, and when the priest had anointed her, she died.

For the motif of a tearless parent at the time of death of the children, see Legend No. 54 in the present volume.

8 Old woman's faith overcomes the Devil

There was a woman in this place, and she was very pious when she was young. You never saw anybody as well-mannered, as gentle or as honest as she. There was a good sky over her head. She was gay and easy-going, likeable and happy in her mind. But the old people used to say that a young, religious person is the makings of an old devil! And there's no lie in that.

According as this woman got on in years, she grew sad and changeable, wrathful and vicious. She attacked everybody she met. She let nobody pass by. But nobody was more greatly to be pitied than her poor husband! It was he who suffered most. Her tongue never stopped attacking him from morning till night and from night till morning, like a windmill that never rested. She wasn't too bad while her health lasted, but when sickness came on her at last, she went to the Devil altogether! Nothing could withstand her. Her poor husband was ruined by her in more ways than one; he spent all he had on her, sending for every doctor and physician he heard of;

each brought along his own kinds of medicines, but they were all useless. They couldn't make her better. If she were a good woman, she would have died long since, but it is hard to kill a bad person! And no matter how ill she was, her tongue was as strong as ever!

There was a beggar travelling around the place, and he was supposed to have some special 'knowledge'. One night he called in to this old couple and asked for lodgings until morning. The old man said that he would be welcome, if he could tell him what was wrong with the old woman. He said that he would do his best. He went to her bed and looked at the old woman, and you may be sure that what she said to him wasn't the best! He stood looking at her for a while, and her tongue going like a windmill, and she scolding him as hard as she could. He listened patiently to her for a long time. At last he shook his head, and then he walked up and down the floor. The old husband asked what he thought of her.

'I don't think much of her!' said he. 'The Devil has gone in between two of her ribs, and it won't be easy to drive him out.'

'Is there any cure for her?' asked the old man.

'There's only one cure,' said the beggar, 'and that cure is far away from here.'

'Tell me what it is,' said the husband, 'and I'll do my best to get it.'

'There's an aspen tree growing in Norway,' said the beggar, 'and if three bits of it could be got and burned under her nose, they would rout the Devil.'

Next morning, a hardy, swift boy of the neighbours was sent off to get the bits of aspen. On his way to the harbour, he came upon a man who was repairing an old boat. They started to chat and, in the conversation, the messenger told him where he was going.

'If I were in your place,' said the boat-man, 'I would shorten my journey. I would bring a handful of the bits of this old boat to the old woman, and they might cure her as well as any other bits you could find!'

The messenger took two or three bits of the wood of the old boat and faced for home. When he thought that he should be back from Norway, he took the bits to the old woman. He asked her to sit up in the bed. She did, and he burned the bits of wood under her nose, and when the last bit was almost burned, the Devil jumped out of her mouth!

'You're a coward, if you were routed by bits of an old boat!' said the messenger.

'Oh! it wasn't the bits of wood that drove me out, but the strong faith of the old hag!' said the Devil.

This legend also may have been used as an *exemplum*.

9 *March cock banishes the Devil*

There were four or five young men, just like the four or five of yourselves tonight, God bless ye! And they went putting bets with one another to see which of them had the best nerve. They were all boasting about what they could do, and there was one of them in it, and 'twas given up to him by all that he was afraid of nothing, living or dead. So the bet they put was that he was to go to the graveyard, like you'd go to Shanaglish graveyard from here, and bring a skull out of it at the dead hour of night.

'That's no bother on me!' says he. 'If I can get the skull, I'll bring it.'

So the bet was put, and when 'twas drawing on the hour of midnight, he started for the graveyard. The other four knew well the time he started, and didn't they start off at the same time and headed for the graveyard. They took a short-cut through the country, and they were landed at the graveyard before him. The four of them went to hide in the corners of the graveyard, the way they wouldn't be seen, and they waited until they saw him coming into the graveyard. In he came, and he went around the tombstones until he'd see who was the longest buried. He came to this one that was hundreds of years old, and he started to dig down with his shovel. 'Twasn't long until he rooted up a fine, big skull, and he held it in his hand. No sooner had he the skull in his hand than the voice spoke from the corner of the graveyard.

'Leave that skull there! That's my grandfather's skull!'

Who was speaking, sure, but one of the lads from a corner!

'Well, if 'tis your grandfather's skull, he can keep it to blazes!' says the fellow.

He went off to another old tombstone and he started to root

away, and the devil a long until he had the second skull in his fist!
The voice spoke again from the corner of the graveyard.

'Leave that skull there! That's my grandfather's skull!'

'Upon my soul, but 'tis strange that 'tis your two grandfathers I
chanced to come across! Let him have it!'

So he started off again until he came to another old tombstone,
and he started rooting away again. 'Twasn't long until he had the
third skull in the heel of his fist.

'Leave that skull there! That's my grandfather's skull!' says the
voice again from the corner of the graveyard.

'Bad luck to you, whoever you are!' says the fellow, 'if it isn't you
that have the three grandfathers! Everyone in the graveyard is your
grandfather, if I could believe you! Anyway, I'm going to bring this
skull with me, and you can take it off me, if you are able!'

So he put the skull inside his coat and made off home. And didn't
the four take the short-cut again, and they were at home before him!
In he came, and he having the skull in his hand, coming in the door.

'You brought it with you.'

'Upon my soul, I did! And if I was to believe the ghosts, I had
no right to take it! One of them was making out that every skull
in the graveyard was his own grandfather's, so I took this one and
told him to take it off me, if he was able, and upon my soul, he
bothered me no more!'

'And what'll you do with the skull now?'

'I'll keep it and respect it, and 'twill be buried along with myself
when I die.'

So he took the skull into the room, where he had what they call
a camp-bed or a canopy-bed, and he left the skull up on top of it.
He was married to his wife about six years at the time, and the Devil
was trying for those six years to come into the house, between the
husband and the wife, and put them quarrelling and fighting.

So this night the Devil came at the hour of midnight and he tried
to come into the house, but as soon as he came as far as the door,
the March cock crew. The Devil was put out on the top of his head
again, and didn't the skull laugh above on the top of the camp-bed!
The cock crew a second time, and didn't the skull laugh again. The
cock crew a third time, and the skull laughed the third time. The
husband and his wife were puzzled, and he went and he took down
the skull off the bed. He held it behind the fire.

'Well,' says he to the skull, 'I'll burn you behind the fire, if you don't tell me the reason of your laugh.'

It was then the skull spoke.

'Well,' says the skull, 'since you asked me, I must tell you. Since the day you married, the Devil has been continually trying to come inside your door to see could he cause trouble between you and your wife, but your cock never let him pass the threshold of your door. He tried to come in tonight again, and, as soon as he landed at your door, the cock crew and flapped his wings and put him out on the top of his head again. I laughed then, I was so delighted to see the Devil getting beat. The Devil faced the door again the second time, and the cock routed him again. I laughed again to see him getting beat the second time. He faced the door for the third time, and the cock crew and routed him, and I laughed again. The Devil went away then and he returned no more. That's the reason why I laughed.'

'Very well,' says the husband to the skull. 'I'll keep you and respect you while I live, and when I'm burying, you'll go down into the same grave with me!'

And he kept his word. The skull was buried in the one grave with him.

A 'March cock' has been described as one born from an egg laid on the first Tuesday in March and hatched out on a Tuesday of the same month. See note in *Folktales of Ireland*, O'Sullivan, 276, as well as the tale, 'The March Cock and the Coffin', 191-2 *ibid*.

Fetching a skull from a graveyard at night often occurs as a test of prowess in oral tradition.

10 *The Devil invented alcoholic drink*

There was a holy man, and word came to him from Heaven that the world was to be flooded. He was told to make an Ark, and he was to tell nobody what he was making as long as he was at it. He started the work. He went off every morning and came back at night; his wife used to ask him where he was, but he wouldn't tell her. It went on like that for seven years. Then one day the Devil came to his wife and asked her where her husband was. She said that she didn't know; he had gone off every morning and come home every night for seven years and wouldn't tell his wife or family where he was or what he was doing.

Then the Devil turned himself into a boar and a lot of froth came from his snout. He told the woman to put some of the froth into her husband's drink that night, and he would tell her what he was doing. It is said that there was no harm in any kind of drink up to that time; it wouldn't make you drunk, any more than water would now. When the man came home that night, the wife put some of the Devil's froth into his drink, and soon after he swallowed it he was drunk. He didn't know where he was, and his talk was vile. He used all kinds of bad words. His wife asked him where he used to spend every day, and he told her everything. When he came to his senses, he knew that something had happened. He went to the Ark, and when he struck the first blow, all the work he had done during the seven years fell to pieces, and the sound of the blow was heard from the eastern world to the western world. Ever since the hammer-blows of a boat-builder are heard further off than any other noise.

He started to build the Ark again, and everybody knew what he was doing. He had it finished just before the world was to be drowned. Then he took a couple of all kinds into the Ark, as he had been told, and he was sailing on and on, and the world being drowned. One day he sent out a raven but it came back again. The man said that the world wasn't drying yet. 'Twas the same the second day. But on the third day, the raven didn't return, so they knew that the world was drying and that the raven would perch on the first bit of dry land it saw, as it had eaten nothing since they started sailing. They sailed on then, and the flood was ebbing, until the Ark landed on top of a mountain in Turkey. It is there still.

For references to the Deluge, Noah and the Ark in ancient literatures, see Frazer, *Folk-lore in the Old Testament,* Vol. I, 104 ff.

11 *Saint Michael wins a soul from the Devil*

There was a wild man there long ago, and he had a very gentle wife.
The poor people and the neighbours were constantly calling to the
house, for they were often short of food. The wild husband thought
that there were too many callers to his good wife, so he gave orders
after a while that she should admit nobody; if she did, he would
shoot them. Faith, she became afraid, and she let nobody in. She
would give them some alms, but they would have to go away then;
they got no lodgings.

A very bad night came, wild and wet and cold. The wild man and
his boy were gone on some journey. Two travelling friars came to
the house, when the bad weather had overtaken them on their
travels, and they could find no other shelter. The woman of the
house gave them food, and told them that she couldn't let them in.

'I'll send ye to the barn at the back,' said she. 'There's straw there
and ye can sleep on it.'

She took them to the barn when they had eaten. The wild man
and his boy came home, and the boy took the horses to the barn. He
heard the sound of breathing there, and came back and told the wild
man about it.

'Is there anyone in the barn?' he asked his wife.

She had no way out but to tell him about the two friars that had
been caught by the bad weather.

'I had to give them some shelter,' she said.

'Bring them here to me!' said he.

They were brought in.

'Now, I'm going to put a bullet through ye!' said the wild man.

'We'll be satisfied with that,' said the older friar, 'but give me time
to deliver a short sermon. You can shoot me then.'

The old friar stood on a table that was there, took off his hat and
started the sermon. The wild man was standing on the floor in front
of him, looking straight into the friar's eyes. He thought that he
could see two angels in the friar's eyes.

'Now, you can put a bullet through me,' said the friar when he
had finished the sermon.

'I won't,' said the wild man. 'I'll get a bed ready for ye.'

He went out to the barn, brought in a huge armful of straw and spread it in the corner. While he was spreading it, tears fell from his eyes and wetted the straw. He put the friars to sleep in the corner. After a while the old friar saw the Devil and Saint Michael on the floor, weighing scales between them, and each of them throwing something on to his own side of the scales.

'He's mine now!' the Devil would say, when he threw something on to his scale.

'He's not! He's still mine!' Saint Michael would say, as he threw in on his own side some good deed the wild man had done, and lifted the Devil's scale high into the air.

Then the Devil would throw something into his own scale and lift Saint Michael's side high up. They were carrying on like that, until the Devil threw in something heavy.

'He's mine now, in spite of you!' said he.

'Not yet!' said Saint Michael.

He took hold of the armful of straw that was under the friars, threw it on his scale and lifted the Devil's side up into the air. The two friars were watching.

'He's mine now, no matter what you do!' said Saint Michael.

The Devil had to give up. While they were arguing, the woman of the house screamed that her husband was dead.

'Don't wonder at that!' said the old friar. 'He's safe and sound in Heaven now. I saw Saint Michael and the Devil here with weighing scales. The straw he put under us in the corner saved his soul for him.'

The 'Saint Michael', who is often mentioned in oral tradition, is apparently the Archangel Michael. As well as being the patron of high places (Mont S. Michel, Sceilg Mhichíl in Kerry), he is often mentioned in folk and other prayers as the defender of human souls against the Devil.

12 *The Devil's cloven foot*

There is an old story that the Devil had every trade excepting carpentering. So one day he went to a carpenter to learn the trade.

The Devil asked the carpenter would he learn him the trade, and the carpenter said that he would. The carpenter gave him overalls and a rule and told him to start to work right away. The Devil was delighted to be learned the trade. The carpenter told him that he never could become a proper carpenter till he was able to use the adze, because it was the tool most used by a carpenter.

The Devil told him to give him the adze and that he would learn to use that before he would learn how to do anything else. The carpenter told him he would give him the adze, so he got a piece of green, tough timber and gave the adze to the Devil and told him to dress the piece of timber. The Devil started to work right away, but he wasn't long at the piece of timber when he split his foot with the adze. When the carpenter saw his foot all destroyed, he told the Devil that he never could be a carpenter after what he had done to his leg, and he couldn't do a better thing than to give up the idea of ever learning that trade, because he had his leg destroyed now, and if he ever again went working an adze, he would do the same thing again to his leg, and he wouldn't be able to walk any more.

The Devil took the carpenter's advice and he never again went learning to be a carpenter. His foot never got back to the right shape again, and that's the reason why he has the cloven hoof to the present day.

Reference to the cloven hooves of the Devil, as cardplayer in human guise, is commonly found in oral tradition in Ireland. See *Volksüberlieferung,* ed. Harkort, Peeters and Wildhaber, Ó Súilleabháin, 277-8. 'The Devil in Irish Folk Narrative'.

III
Origins

Aetiological legends seek to explain the origins of various things. They are often fanciful and do not pretend to give true reasons to account for how particular things came into being. They are, however, based on a kind of keen observation of nature and of other facets of life.

13 *The cat and the dog*

There was a saint in Inishglora long ago, and one day he was going through the island to bless it. It wasn't long till he met a fine, handsome woman – you would think that she was the Beauty of the Sun! The saint had a grain of clay in his hand and he was about to sprinkle it on the island to bless it, when the woman spoke to him:

'If you throw away what you have in your hand, I'll marry you.'

The saint paused and thought for a long while. He looked to every side, and when he looked at the woman, he saw that she had hooves like those of a cow. He knew then that she wasn't a woman of this world but an evil spirit. He immediately raised his hand and banished her out on the strand to a rock which is now called the Rock of the Women. She was seen no more there because she was the Devil's mother.

She left the place then and kept on going when she had failed to tempt the saint. At last she was within three miles of Dublin. Very well! She met a man there then and asked him to marry her. He thought that she was the finest woman that human eye had ever seen and, therefore he noticed nothing about her which was different from any other woman. He promised to marry her and he did. Time passed, and he had a son and a daughter by her. He was a farmer. One day he was reaping oats with his son – it was at the time when Saint Patrick came to Ireland. That same day, Saint Patrick passed by the place and started to chat with them, telling them who he was. Soon after, they were called to their dinner, and the father told the son that he should stay in the field to protect the oats from the birds of the air, until he and the saint returned.

'Oh!' said Saint Patrick, 'there is no need for any of ye to stay here. The birds won't touch it, I promise ye that!'

They took the saint's advice, and the three of them went off to the dinner. When they reached the house, there was a fish boiling for them, and when it was boiled, it was put on the table for them. After a while the saint noticed that the woman had assumed a very evil appearance. She was very silent. When the fish was placed in front of them, the saint made the Sign of the Cross over it. They ate and drank their fill and then went out again. The saint remained with the family all day, and he finally said to the husband:

'Do you notice any difference between your wife and other women?'

'No,' said he.

'She is the Devil's mother, wherever you met her!'

'God save us!' said the husband. 'Is it possible to banish her?'

'It is, if you agree,' said the saint.

'I'd agree to anything, if I could get rid of her,' said the husband.

'Well,' said the saint, 'I'll go home with ye again tonight. I'll pretend nothing, but when she goes to bed, I'll banish her.'

The three of them returned home in the evening. They were chatting and didn't feel the time passing. When they went to bed, the saint stood up and banished her from the house in a ball of flame. As she went out, she knocked down the side-wall.

'What will you do with her two children?' asked the man.

'I won't do the same to them,' said the saint. 'I'll leave them to be of service to the people.'

He changed the daughter into a cat and the son into a dog, and it is said that this is the reason why those two animals have a kind of human nature ever since. They will be that way for ever.

I don't know whether it is true or a lie, but it has been going around on the lips of people who are alive now, and of those who lived before them as well.

For a different story to explain how cats and mice came into the world, see Richmond (ed), *Studies in Folklore,* Ó Súilleabháin, 252-26, 'The Feast of Saint Martin in Ireland'. Inishglora and 'The Rock of the Women' (Carraig na mBan) are off the coast of County Mayo. The Devil's mother (An Chaorthanach) is often mentioned as an evil character in Irish oral tradition.

14 *The plaice and the salmon*

It is said that it was Saint Patrick who gave the salmon its power to jump, and it was he who twisted the mouth of the plaice. It happened in this way.

When Saint Patrick was travelling through Ireland, he baptised a

great many people, but others who were pagans wouldn't yield to
him at all. One day when he was going along, he passed by a river
where some men were fishing. They were pagans and they wanted to
make some kind of fun of the saint. As Patrick was passing by, one
of the fishermen shouted:

'Wait, Patrick, and you'll get a fish!'

'I will,' said Patrick.

He sat down by the river. Soon afterwards one of the fishermen
pulled up a huge fish, but if he did he didn't give it to Patrick. He
threw it into the basket along with the other fish. Patrick stood up
and he was about to walk away, when another of the pagans spoke.

'Wait, Patrick, and you'll get the next fish we catch!'

'I will, indeed!' said Patrick.

He sat down again. Soon they pulled up another fish; they didn't
give it to Patrick but threw it into the basket again. Patrick got up
and was about to go away, when a third pagan said:

'Wait, Patrick, and you'll get the next fish we catch!'

'I will, of course!' said Patrick.

He sat down again on a high hummock some distance from the
river. The first fish that they caught was a plaice. Until that time, the
head of the plaice was as straight on its body as was the head of every
other fish, but when the plaice saw how the pagans were mocking
the saint, it wished to take part in the mockery also. It gave a turn
to its own neck and twisted its mouth and looked backwards over
its shoulder insultingly. When Patrick saw that it was grimacing
towards himself,

'May your head remain as it is!' said he.

And it did! The plaice was unable to get rid of its twisted neck
and head, and they have remained so ever since. When Patrick was
about to get up off the hummock, a salmon leaped cleanly out of the
middle of the river and landed on Saint Patrick's breast.

'I give you the gift of jumping!' said the saint.

And ever since, the salmon can jump better than any other fish,
and that will be so until the end of time.

For references to the flounder's crooked mouth, see Dähnhardt,
Natursagen III, 24, IV, 192-7; Bolte and Polivka, *Anmerkungen*, III,
284; *FFC*, VIII, 21, XXXVII, 89, LXVI, 91. For the salmon's
swimming powers, see Dähnhardt, *ibid*. III, 222; for the legend of the
salmon's leap, see Szövérffy, *Irisches Erzählgut*, 123.

15 *The harp*

There was a chieftain who lived near the sea long ago, himself and his wife, and she was very fond of singing and music. One day a dead whale was washed ashore by the tide, and the carcase remained on the shore until it rotted away and nothing was left but the skeleton.

When the wind used to blow through the skeleton of the whale, it made lovely music. And the chieftain's wife made an instrument with strings out of the whale. Thus the harp was invented.

For references to the making of the harp in imitation of the whale's skeleton, see Irish Texts Society, *Lebor Gabála Érenn,* I, 89, 159; 'Celtic', in MacCulloch, *Mythology of All Races,* III, 137; Ossianic Society Transactions, V, 97 ff; Wood-Martin, *Traces of the Elder Faiths in Ireland,* I, 180 f.

16 *The lark's march*

Well, 'tis often I heard that it happened this way. There was a dance one night in a house, and two pipers were invited there. A challenge was laid as to which of the two was the best. They were the whole night playing music. They played every second round, and one of them had played all the tunes he knew. The two were sitting on two chairs set on two tables. And this piper who had no other tune did not know what to do. It was his turn to start again when the other piper stopped playing. He had no other tune and he knew that the other piper would win the challenge.

He laid his pipes down on the chair and went out into the street. Day was dawning. And what happened to be outside but a lark, singing for herself! He listened to her and learned the tune she was singing: the Lark's March. When he went into the house again, he went up on the table. He had to start again, and the only tune he had was the Lark's March, that he had heard the lark singing outside. He took hold of the pipes and played the Lark's March for them. The other piper had no new tune and he lost the challenge. It was the

lark that directed the winner. Wasn't he a good piper to pick up the
tune from her? It has been played ever since.

As a corollary to this story, there is in Ireland a legend which tells
how the lark flew so high that she reached Heaven's gate and brought
back the beautiful music which she had heard there.
Contests in skill between musicians of various kinds are often
described in Irish oral tradition.

17 *The love of a mother*

Saint Joseph and the Virgin Mary were walking through a glen one
day, and the Holy Virgin heard a great noise coming towards them.
The Child Jesus was with them.

'Take care, Son!' said the Virgin. 'Do you hear that noise coming
towards us in the glen?'

'You're in no danger, Mother,' said the Son of God. 'My own
Father will protect us.'

'Oh, you are my seven loves, Son!' said she.

'Mother,' said He, 'you have left a bad gift to the mothers of the
world! Every mother will have seven loves for her son against the
one love he will have for her!'

They say that is why each mother has seven loves for her son.

Apocryphal legends of this kind are very common in Ireland, and are
generally associated with Our Saviour or the Virgin Mary. They seek
to explain how certain things came about in the first instance.

18 *The Jews and Our Saviour*

When the Son of God was walking the earth with His mother, he
was going along one day and there were three Jews on the road.
When they saw Him coming, one of them said to the others: 'Here
now is the Son of God and His mother, and we'll see has He any
miracles'.

They had a large barrel at the edge of the road. They put one of themselves under it, and the other two waited until the Son of God came up to them. They spoke and, after a while, one of the Jews asked the Son of God what was under the barrel. He said that there was a pig, The two Jews started to laugh. After a while they lifted up the barrel, and what ran out from under it but a young pig! When they saw that, they said nothing. They knew well then that it was the Son of God was there and that he had miracles.

They said that they would believe in all He said from that time on. That was all right. But from that day to this no Jew has eaten a bite of pig-flesh, fearing that it would belong to the pig under the barrel.

Tom Peete Cross's *Motif-Index of Early Irish Literature* does not mention the relevant motif (A1681.2), but Stith Thompson's *Motif-Index* gives a number of references to it in European sources. Legends containing disagreeable racial elements are commonplace in most countries. The stereotype associating Jew and pig is unpleasant, since it mocks the religious practice of others. It is common in medieval sculpture, as well as in the later graphic arts, and in modern times it was employed in Nazi propaganda. See Isaiah Shachar, *The Judensau: A Medieval Anti-Jewish Motif and its History* (the Warburg Institute; London, 1974).

19 *The seven penitential psalms*

There was a king there long ago, and he had ninety-nine wives, one short of a hundred. His son was married and had his own wife. But the old father didn't know what plan to carry out in order to get the son's wife along with the rest! The son knew well that his father had that notion, and he went to speak to him one day.

' 'Tis a strange story I have for you,' said he to his father. 'There's a gentleman in a certain place,' naming the place, 'and he has a hundred sheep, except one. A very poor man is living across the boundary from him, and the only wordly thing or substance he has is a single sheep. But the gentleman wants to take that sheep from

him to join all that he has already! I'm asking you now, father,' said
the son, 'what had best be done to the man who wants to take the
poor man's sheep along with all he has already.'

The king thought for a while and said:

'That man deserves to be buried seven fathoms under ground.'

'Well,' said the son, 'you are that man! You want to take my wife
from me to put her with the ninety-nine others that you have
already.'

Small wonder! He had given the judgement on himself and he
had to obey it. A hole seven fathoms deep was dug and the king was
buried in it. He started to make seven psalms, and he rose up a
fathom for every psalm. The seventh psalm brought him to the
surface of the earth.

The king and his son, who are mentioned but not named in the
present version, are David and Solomon in most others. Solomon
figures as the wise and just man in a number of Irish stories. The
motif T161 *Jus primae noctis* (by which a tyrant claims a tenant's wife
on her wedding night) is often connected with this story in other
versions.

20 *The fairies*

This is what caused the war in Heaven. The Eternal Father had a
parlour, and no angel had permission to enter it. Lucifer was the
highest of all the angels. He looked into the room when he got a
chance. The Mirror of Glory was inside and it showed a picture of
the Glorious Virgin, who wasn't to come into the world for another
two thousand years. That's what caused the war in Heaven; if Lucifer
hadn't done what he did, there would be no war there. Some took
the side of God and others the side of Lucifer.

They say that at that time, the sun and the moon and everything
could talk. The sun backed God and was left to continue giving
light as before. The moon backed Lucifer, and it was reduced from
its prime to a slender silken thread, and then back and fro to full size
again. The sea backed Lucifer too. It was steady until that time, but
God sent it back, six hours ebbing and six hours flowing and
striking itself against the rocks.

The bad angels were sent out from Heaven, and no thicker shower of snow has fallen from that day to this than the shower of angels leaving Heaven. When God was asked not to empty Heaven, He said:

'As it is now, let it remain!'

Those angels that had reached the earth are still on the earth; and those that had not reached the earth are still going around in the skies, in gusts and blasts of wind – we call them the *Slua le Doininn* (the fairy host). The chief angel, the Devil we call him, is in a hole, and he cannot move until a human tongue calls him.

When the Eternal Father had done that much, He was angry, and He closed Heaven for two thousand years. Everyone who died during that time went to Limbo.

The myth enshrined in this legend which seeks to explain how the fairies originated is very well known in Irish oral tradition. It also seeks to explain the causes of the moon's phases, and how the fairies came to live in the so-called 'fairy forts' (abandoned homesteads of former times). The *'Slua le Doininn' (Slua sí:* fairy host) mentioned in the text were the most feared of the fairies as they went around among humans trying to take some of them into the fairy world.

In some of the versions, it was Michael the Archangel who pleaded with God not to 'empty Heaven' by banishing all of the rebellious angels.

21 *Why the fairies are vindictive*

There was a man living in Ballynabo at the end of the bad times. His name was Sean Magee. He was taken ill suddenly one night, and the priest had to be sent for. The parish Priest was up when the call came and he sent for the curate. He got out of bed, but he thought it too lonely to go out by himself, so he asked the parish priest to go with him. The two of them set out on foot, walking quickly towards Ballynabo. As they were walking down the hillside towards Carrowcannon, a man with bagpipes came out on the road ahead of them, and he went along before them playing the pipes. They followed him until they reached the bridge at Rath. They were surprised, no doubt, to see a piper on the road in front of them so late at night, but they liked his music and didn't feel tired or lonely when they came to the bridge. The parish priest put his hand into his pocket for some money to give to the piper.

'I don't want even a halfpenny of money,' said the piper.

'We liked your music and we want to reward you for it,' said the parish priest.

'If you would,' said the piper, 'you can do this for me. When Sean is dying tonight, ask him where will I go on the Last Day.'

The parish priest was surprised at this.

'I'll ask him the question all right,' said he, 'but what name will I call you?'

'Just say: "The piper" '.

'Very well,' said the parish priest.

The piper went on ahead of them again, up through Rath, playing his fine music till they reached the gable of Sean's house. Although he had been with them up to then, the two priests completely forgot about the piper when they went inside the house. Sean was very weak. The priest anointed him, and they stayed a good while in the house. When they left to go home, the parish priest saw a dark figure near an elder tree, and he immediately remembered the piper. He returned to the house and asked Sean the question. Sean wasn't a bit surprised at that, but he turned around in the bed and said:

'If he can find enough blood in his body with which to write his name, he'll go to Heaven!'

The priests left the house again, and the piper went in front of them until they reached the bridge again. There he waited for them.

'Well, what did he say?' he asked.

'He said that if you can find enough blood in your body with which to write your name, you will go to Heaven.'

The piper threw down his pipes, pulled a penknife from his pocket, and stabbed himself in the breast. But not a drop of blood came out! He stabbed himself again and again, but all that came out was froth like the froth on a river.

'Who are you, poor man?' asked the priest. 'Where have you come from?'

'I'm a fairy who has been going about since the beginning of time. I have never harmed anyone, but I'll do nothing but harm from now on, seeing that Heaven is not in store for me!'

He vanished from their sight in flashes of fire! The priests returned home, full of wonder. From that night on, they never saw the piper again, nor did they find out how Sean knew what would happen to the fairy on the Day of Judgement.

> The more usual version of this story tells how a man who had fallen out with the priest spent each Sunday walking on the mountain; here he met a stranger who asked him to go to the local church where Mass was being celebrated and to ask the priest at the time of Consecration (when the priest, according to the story, had to answer) what three types of persons would not get into Heaven on the Last Day. In the supposed reply of the priest, the types vary, but the fairies are always one of them. The bearer of the verdict was saved from the fury of the fairies by lying in a grave-like hole over which a spade and shovel were laid in the form of a cross. The fairies, who are said to be bloodless try to get some blood by abducting humans into their world.
>
> The townlands mentioned are in County Donegal.

22 *The man in the moon*

I never heard that the man in the moon was a thresher, but I heard them saying that he was a man that went out one night and stole a bush. And when he was coming home with the bush on his shoulder, God made an example of him and put him up in the moon, the way that everyone could see the punishment he got for stealing. There was plenty of people believed that that was the case, and they'd say: 'Look at the man in the moon with the bush on his shoulder' or 'the man in the moon with the bush in his hand'. People would be telling that to children to warn them against stealing anything, and how they would be punished for it. They'd point up at the man in the moon and say that he'd be there till the Day of Judgement as a punishment for his sin.

> This legend is of a mythical character which seeks to explain the origin of the darkened area on the face of the moon, and is also didactic in its moral teaching.

23 *Why mowers are poor*

There was a poor mower in Ireland long ago. He had a large family and no means of supporting them except mowing a field of hay here and there. He was paid accordingly. He was hired one Saturday night to mow a field and, so poor was he, he went out to start the work on Sunday morning. He thought that he could do this without being seen, as the field was far off behind a hill. On his way he met a fine-looking man.

'Where are you going today?' asked the stranger.

The mower told him that he was going mowing as he needed money.

'Isn't this Sunday?' said the stranger.

'I know it is, but that can't be helped.'

'How much would you earn by today's work?'

'Six shillings.'

'Well, this is Sunday,' said the stranger. 'Here are six shillings for you, and go back home!'

The mower took the six shillings and turned towards home. After he had gone a short distance, he thought to himself:

'If I had the money I'd earn today along with these six shillings, I'd be well off.'

He turned around and soon met another man who asked him where he was going. He told him he needed money badly.

'How much would you get for today's mowing?' asked the stranger.

'Six shillings.'

'Well, this is Sunday. Here are six shillings for you. Go back home!'

He turned back, and when he was near his home, he thought to himself again:

'If I had today's pay along with these twelve shillings, I'd be a rich man! I'll turn back.'

He did so. At the same spot, he met a third stranger.

'Where are you going today?' he asked.

'Mowing.'

'Isn't this Sunday?' said the stranger.

'I know it is, but that won't ease my poverty.'

'How much would you earn today?'

'Six shillings,' said the mower.

'Well, here are six shillings for you, and don't let me see you crossing over this hill again! I ordain that all mowers in the world will ever be poor'.

The three strangers were all the same man. That's what left every mower poor ever since!

Legends, possibly of the nature of *exempla,* about punishment meted out to those who break the Sabbath, are found in many countries. *Cf.* No. 53 in the present volume. Some Irish variants explain the supposed poverty of mowers by saying that, in the course of their work, they destroy plants and herbs of a beneficial character in folk medicine.

24 *Sand as fertiliser*

Long ago when there was no law in the country and the strongest was on top, bands of men used to go about robbing and taking away all that they could find.

One day a band of men came down the Conor Pass to seize cattle and take them off. They came as far as Garfinny, at the foot of the hill, and drove the cattle before them. Word was brought to one house that their stock was being taken, but the only person at home was a servant girl. She ran out in great anger, taking with her a large knife to defend her master's property. She was in a rage when she saw what was going on, and stood in front of the rievers at each gap. She stabbed a few of them with the knife, but it was taken from her finally, and she had to stop.

Some time later, she left the farmer and set out to look for work. She got lodgings one night in North Kerry. The man of the house was generous, and he told her to sit down and eat her fill. While she was eating, he asked her did she recognise the knife on the table. She said that she did, and he said that she had shown great bravery the day she had tried to defend the cattle near Dingle.

'They are fine strands ye have west there,' said the man, 'if ye only knew the richness that is in them.'

'How is that ?' she asked.

'We often noticed,' said he, 'that wherever a dog lay down, and he covered with sand after rolling himself on the strand, a fine crop of grass would grow there.'

That's how the people here found out that sand improves the land.

> The rieving of cattle (*creach*) was of common occurrence in former times in Ireland, where the animals took the place of our modern money. The use of white sea-sand, as well as of sea-weed, was one of the mainstays for fertilising the land of farms near the coast.
>
> The Conor Pass, Garfinny and Dingle are in the Dingle Peninsula of West Kerry.

25 *How women got an excuse*

When Our Saviour and His Mother were travelling about long ago, He was starting to perform miracles at that time. They were walking along the road and met a blind man who was sitting at the side of it. When they passed by him, the Virgin Mother remarked that the man was blind.

'He is,' said Our Saviour. 'And even so, there is his wife in that wood over there along with another man. I'm going to give the blind man his sight so that he can see her.'

'If you do,' said His Mother, 'give the woman an excuse.'

No sooner did He say the word than the blind man rose to his feet and looked around in all directions. He looked towards the wood and saw his wife. She knew that he had seen her and she came towards him. When she came near,

'You were in the wood with that man ' said he.

'If I hadn't been there, you wouldn't have got back your sight !' said the wife.

And that's how all women have got an excuse from that day to this !

> This is one of several aetiological stories found in Ireland which attempt to explain the origin of some human characteristics.
>
> Compare Chaucer's use of this motif in *The Merchant's Tale*.

26 *Saint John's Eve bonfires*

Long ago, under the old law, when John the Baptist was beheaded at the woman's request, the head was thrown out on a fence. It was there for some days when a Jewish girl was on her way to the well one day and she took pity on it.

'I pity your head there !' said she.

The skull spoke and said :

'Still more are you a pity, breaking the rules of the Sabbath !'

The girl ran into the house and screamed that the skull on the fence had spoken. Orders were given immediately to take and burn it. That was done ; it was burned. And such a fine crop never grew since as came from the portion of land over which the smoke passed !

Because of that, bonfires have been lighted on Saint John's Eve ever since to this day, and even today.

Bonfires are still commonly lighted in Ireland on certain festivals (May Eve, Hallowe'en, and especially on the Eve of the Feast of Saint John, 23 June). Cattle are driven close to the fires or between two of them to ward off diseases, and some of the burning bushes or embers are thrown into the fields where crops are growing, to safeguard them against diseases and to stimulate their growth.

27 *Lough Neagh*

They say Lough Neagh was formed this way. A mother went for a can of water and she left her child in the cradle. The child started to cry, or the house went on fire, and the woman ran to her child. She left the well uncovered, and the well overflowed, and she could not go back to cover it. So the whole valley was filled with water and made Lough Neagh.

Legends to explain how lakes came to be formed when a well overflowed are very common in Ireland. Lough Neagh is the largest lake in Ireland ; its eastern shore reaches to within a dozen miles of Belfast.

IV

The Supernatural

Mankind has generally believed in the existence of a more-or-less invisible world, close to our material world and peopled by beings—gods, devils, demons, spirits, the dead, fairies and others. This otherworld, in pre-Christian times, had little, if any, resemblance to later ideas of God, Heaven, Purgatory or Hell. For example, there was no strict line to be observed between the world of the fairies and that of the dead. Imagination went riot, and even the under-water world was as well-populated as the dry land. Some of the finest Irish legends are to be found in this Section.

28 'Pan is dead'

There was a man named Walter living here in this townland. He was going to buy shoes for his children one day. The previous day a strange cat had come into the house. This cat was sitting by the fire and he overheard Walter talking about the shoes.

'Walter,' said he, 'bring a pair of shoes for me too !'

'I will,' said Walter.

Walter grew afraid of the cat when he heard him speak. He didn't go for the shoes at all, but instead went to a man who had a pack of hounds and told him his story.

'Meet me at the crossroads tomorrow morning at ten o'clock,' said the man of the hounds. 'Bring the cat with you in a sack, and I'll settle him !'

Walter went home without any shoes.

'You didn't bring the shoes, Walter,' said the cat.

'I didn't,' said Walter. 'He'll have to take your measure tomorrow.'

When Walter rose next morning, he put the cat into a sack to take him to the shoemaker to get measured. He wasn't long at the crossroads when the man with the pack of hounds came.

'What have you in the sack, Walter ?' he asked.

'Oh, nothing much,' said Walter.

'There's something in it,' said the man. 'Open it till I have a look.'

'Don't, for the life of you, Walter ! Don't open it !' said the cat.

'Open it till I see what's inside !' said the man of the hounds.

Walter opened the sack. Out ran the cat, and the hounds attacked and killed it. When the cat was dying, it said :

'You shouldn't have done that, Walter ! You shouldn't have done it ! When you go home, tell Crónán Beside the Fire that you killed the Son of Big Anna.'

Walter returned home.

'Did you get rid of the cat ?' asked his wife.

'I did. I had to. And the cat told me to tell Crónán Beside the Fire that I have killed the Son of Big Anna.'

His own cat that was beside the fire jumped up and attacked Walter in the throat. Only for stopping him, he would have killed Walter.

This legend about the supernatural cat which seeks to avenge the death of a fellow cat is an echo in oral tradition of the myth which tells how, on the day that Christ was crucified, the crew of a ship which was passing the island of Naxos in the Mediterranean heard a call from the island : 'Great Pan is dead !' When the ship reached Rome, the story was told, and it was noted that henceforth all the oracles were silent.

For various studies made of this tale, see the bibliography given by Thompson, *Motif-Index*, motif F442.1 'Mysterious voice announces death of Pan', to which add *Studia Fennica* III, 6 (1938) Martti Haavio, 'Der Tod des grossen Pan'. For Plutarch's first century version of the legend see av Klintberg, *Svenska Folksägner*, 7, 132-4.

29 *The monk and the bird*

The old people used to tell a story about a priest who was going to say Mass one Sunday morning in some chapel out in the country. He had put on his vestments, but the congregation which he expected hadn't yet arrived.

'I won't say Mass for some minutes to see will more people turn up,' said he to himself.

There was a kind of small wood near the chapel. He heard music like the singing of a bird there, and went to the door and looked in that direction. He moved out a little to see if he could lay eyes on the bird that was singing. He caught sight of it, and its beauty and music was greater than he had ever experienced. The bird left its perch and flew off a little way. It began to sing again. The priest was so desirous of seeing and hearing it that he followed it for another little while. Then he remembered his congregation.

'They'll be gathered now' said he, 'and I'll say Mass for them.'

He turned back towards the chapel. There was no congregation waiting for him - only an old man who was doing some kind of work nearby.

'Where are the people who were coming to Mass here ?' the priest asked.

'I don't know anything about them. I didn't see any people,' said the old man.

'I left them here a few minutes ago,' said the priest. 'I wonder where they have gone to.'

'I don't know anything about them either,' said the old man. 'But there's a great story about a priest who was here a couple of hundred years ago. He went out on a Sunday morning, wearing his Mass vestments, and he never came back since. Nobody knows where he went to.'

When the priest heard these words, he became a very old, decrepit man, and he died without delay.

This story used to be among the people, and they used to say that he didn't return because he was wearing the Mass vestments when he followed the bird. They couldn't say whether the bird was from Heaven or whether it might have been some evil kind of bird that wished to harm the priest.

For many studies of this beautiful legend, and references to it, see the bibliography given by Stith Thompson, *Motif-Index*, motif D2011.1.1. The sudden ageing of the priest on his return from listening to the bird's song is reminiscent of that of Oisín when he touched Irish soil on returning from his sojourn in Tír na n-Óg (Land of Youth).

30 *The sleeping warrior*

The old people and the storytellers used to say that there was a man buried in a part of County Clare, near Black Head, and that his tomb was eighteen feet long, with a large, wide, flat stone on top of it. He was said to be under a spell, and his body hadn't decayed or changed in any way since he had been alive on his feet. They said that he would remain there until the Day of Judgement unless he swallowed three drops from a bottle which lay beside his head. His sword lay at his side in the tomb. This story went around among the neighbours and all over the country from one generation to the next.

Some young people in the place said that they would turn the flagstone that was over the tomb to see if the story was true. One day ten or twelve of them went to where the warrior was said to be buried and turned the stone. He was there, as had been said, a bottle near his head and a sword by his side. They took up the bottle and let a drop of what was in it fall into the warrior's mouth. He stirred himself, and the ground shook for about a hundred yards all around. The young men were so frightened that they turned back the stone again and ran off.

He has been there ever since, and will be until the Day of Judgement unless three drops from the bottle are put into his mouth. The young men thought that it might be better to leave him as he was ; it wasn't certain whether good or ill would result, if he rose up. If he did, it might be impossible to kill him with any weapon if he came back to life as he had been before the spell was put on him. He might kill everybody in Ireland.

For the very numerous widespread versions of this legend, see the bibliography given by Stith Thompson, *Motif-Index,* motif D1960.2; also Tom Peete Cross, *Motif-Index of Early Irish Literature,* motif A571. See also *Louth Archaeological Journal,* 14 (1958), 68-81, D. MacIomhair, 'The Legend of Gearóid Iarla of Hacklim'.

31 *Melusine : the otherworld wife*

One of the earls had a castle long ago below here at Carnboy. All of his people had died, and he was living alone. He was a gentle, educated, kindly, honest man. He owned an estate and was well-off for gold and silver ; in a word, he was 'sitting warmly'. He did not marry, for he said that he had never met a girl whom he liked that much.

There was a spring-water well beside the castle. People didn't make much use of it, for they said that a young, handsome girl was living in a cave near the well. She was seen early in the morning and late in the evening going to the well for water. The gentleman thought that the story was a silly one, until one day when he was out hunting. Thunder and heavy rain came on, and he took shelter until it stopped. So it was towards night when he reached the castle. Whom should he see leaving the well but the girl, and he thought that he had never seen her like, she was so beautiful ! He ran after her and caught her before she could reach the cave.

'May I ask you,' said he, 'what is your name and where do you live ?'

'You may,' said she. 'I am the Queen of Loneliness and I live at Carnboy.'

'Wouldn't it be better for you and myself to live together and we could get rid of the loneliness ?' said he.

'I'm agreeable to that,' said she, 'on one condition.'

'What is that ?'

'You mustn't invite any friends, men or woman, to Carnboy as long as I am there,' said she. 'I must always be the Queen of Loneliness. Isn't it hard for you to cut yourself off from the big world for my sake ? Think well now about it, for being sorry too late is not good.'

'I'm prepared to put up with my share of loneliness, and why not ?' said he.

They got married next day. The gentleman kept his promise and invited nobody to the house, nor did he or his wife visit any of the neighbours. They were happy. Neither of them deceived the other and there never was an uncivil word between them. They had two nice children, a son and a daughter. The boy was like his father and the girl like her mother. Time went by and the years brought no change. They were as happy as ever.

The gentleman was growing tired of his life, however, and he was anxious to mix with the people again. There were to be horse-races on the White Strand, and he told his wife the previous day that he would take his race-horse there.

'That's all right,' said she, 'but if you love me and Carnboy, come home by yourself !'

He went off to the races with his horse next morning. The horse won. The same happenened next day and the next; the horse won first prize. The gentleman was delighted. The people gathered around him, and one of them said that his wife would be proud when she heard the good news.

'She will, if he has a wife at all!' said a second man.

'I have the most beautiful wife in the world,' said the gentleman.

'Show her to us, and we'll believe you !'

The gentleman became angry.

'Come with me, and see her !' said he.

The men followed him to his door. He had forgotten all about his promise, until he saw her standing beside the well with the two children at her side. He raced towards her to tell her about the races, but he was late. Before he reached her, she jumped into the well along with the children. None of them was seen from that day to this.

Great sorrow came over him for having broken his promise, and the men were sad too for they were to blame. Before they had any time to talk, however, the water rose high in the well, and they had to flee. The water spread all around and covered all the land nearby. When day dawned, the castle was covered with water, and a great lake that is still there was formed. People who know say that when a clear day comes, the shadow of the castle can be seen under the water, and that three swans swim to and fro over the lake.

The gentleman spent the rest of his life in sadness. He attended to his own affairs and turned his back to the women of the world.

This legend is often referred to as the story of Melusine, the heroine of a local legend attached to the house of Lusignan of France and embodying the tabu against offending a supernatural wife. For studies of the legend and for references to it, see Stith Thompson, *Motif-Index*, motif C31 ; also Tom Peete Cross, *Motif-Index of Early Irish Literature*, under the same motif. The present version is associated with Carnboy in the Parish of Templecrone, County Donegal ; for a somewhat similar version, see No. 91 in the present volume, where the locale is Lake Inchiquin in County Clare.

32 *The door in the cliff*

There is a hill in the parish of Clanlawrence in Béarra in West Cork, and it is called the Cairt. There's a very high, steep cliff at the foot of it, and on its face there is a red patch like a doorway. So it is called the Comhla (doorway).

Anyway, the old people say that there was a *meitheal* (work-group) of men cutting turf one day at the foot of this cliff. Out in the day, their dinner wasn't being brought to them, and they were very hungry. One of them, a young fellow, faced the Comhla, and said:

'Woman of the Comhla, send out our dinner to us!'

The words were barely out of his mouth when the rock opened, and out came a beautiful young woman and a servant girl. They came towards the men, and the woman laid a table-cloth on the grass. She placed all kinds of food and drink on it and told them to start eating. Faith, they all did, except the young fellow who had spoken first; he was afraid to sit down with them. They ate and drank their fill. The woman then gathered up what was left, and went off into the rock again along with the girl. The Comhla closed after them.

A month from that day, the young fellow was in his grave.

This didactic legend warns that when food is demanded and supplied, it must be eaten. See motif C288, Thompson, *Motif-Index*.

33 *The dance of the dead*

For a long time I have been listening to the old people telling about the man who was going to the fair at Ballydehob long ago to buy a cow. He didn't know what time it was when he was leaving the house, because a fox had taken off a fine March cock that they had a short while before. It was a fine, starry night, with no moon.

He was alone, and he had about fifteen or sixteen miles of a journey ahead of him. He went on about ten or twelve miles where he was a stranger and didn't know anyone who lived there. As he was passing a house by the side of the road, he heard very fine, sweet music being played inside. He stopped to listen. He saw light in the house, and he could hear a lot of people dancing on the floor. The dance and music attracted him, for he had a light heart. He went to the door and knocked. It was opened for him and he went in. There was a fine, large kitchen, bursting with people, young men and women dancing. A fairly elderly man was sitting by the fire playing a fiddle for them.

This man who was going to the fair was a very fine dancer himself. He couldn't keep his feet from moving, so he took a quiet, graceful girl who was seated near the door by the hand and took her out on the floor. After the dance he bowed and thanked her and took her back to her seat. He drew himself aside, for there was a huge crowd dancing together on the floor. He was wondering where they had all come from. He stood watching the dance. He had never seen anything like it or heard such fine music. When he got a chance after a while, he gave a groat to the fiddler, and when the next dance started, he slipped out by the door. He said to himself, as he left, that he would try to find out more about these people when he would be on his way back from the fair in daylight. He didn't forget to put a mark opposite the house on the other side of the road, so that he would find the house on his return.

Off he went then to the fair and bought a cow. He then ate his breakfast to face the road home. He left Ballydehob at ten o'clock in the morning, driving the cow before him. He kept an eye on the places he passed through. The houses were few and far between. He asked everyone he met had any of them been at the dance last night in a certain house in such a place. He asked them who was the fiddler. But none of them knew anything about such a dance, and there hadn't been a fiddler in the district for many years. He was told, however, that the old people had heard of a great fiddler who was there long ago, who used to play music in a dancing-school in a house by the side of the road. But he had been dead for forty years or more, and a new house had been built on the site of the dancing-school; a married couple lived there now.

That's what the people he met along the road on his way home told him. At last he reached the house where he had seen the dance the previous night, and he recognised it easily. The door was wide open. He left the cow to graze along the road and went in. The woman of the house was within. She asked him about the fair, and then he asked her about the dance and the dancers she had the night before. He also enquired about the fiddler and where he lived. The woman didn't reply for a while, for she thought that he had either 'a drop taken' or else was a bit 'off his head'.

' 'Tis a long time since there has been a dance in this house,' said she. 'There used to be a dancing-school long ago where this is standing now; that's over forty years ago. The old people, who used to dance there when they were young men and women, say that there was no beating the fiddler who used to play for them.'

He listened to her till she had finished.

'Come outside a minute with me,' said he to her.

She followed him out, and he led her across the road. He put his hand into a hole in the fence and pulled out two socks.

'Do you see those two socks?' he asked.

'I do.'

He then told her the whole story about the dance in her house the night before and how he had put his two socks into the hole in the fence so that he would know the house again on his way home. He told her about the dancers and how he had given a groat to the great fiddler they had.

'Now what do you think of all that?' he asked.

'The greatest surprise of all that I got,' said she, 'was when I found a groat on the chair near the fire when I was 'reddening' it this morning. I was the first up in the house, and it was I who took the bolt off the door and opened it. When I asked my husband had he left the coin on the chair, he said that someone had been playing a trick on me.'

'Now you know how the groat came to be on the chair,' said he.

'I have ever been hearing that "they" are there,' said she.

This well-told legend comes from West Cork where, as in most other parts of Ireland, belief in revenants was very strong. The finding later on of the coin which had been offered to the dead musician adds a piquant touch to the reality of the story.

34 *Dead couple marry after death*

Long ago there was a boy and a girl and they were in love with each other. They had been walking out together for five or six years and the boy had promised to marry her. That was all right until a second girl came home from America. She had a good lot of money, and didn't the boy turn his back on the first girl and go about with the other. When the first girl saw what was happening, she became heart-broken and died. That was that. Before the day on which he was to marry the second girl came, some kind of sickness came on him and he died.

Seven years after that there was a wedding in the next townland, and all the local boys and girls went to it. A young man was on his way to the wedding at night, and his shoes needed mending. He went to the house of a shoemaker at the side of the street and asked him would he mend his shoes.

'I will. Take them off,' said the shoemaker.

He slipped off the shoes, and it was late at night by the time they were mended. He set out then for the wedding-house. He took a short-cut by the side of a hill. The night was fine and bright. He saw a white ghost coming down the hill towards him, and he stopped to look. When the ghost came near him at the other side of a fence, the young man asked him was he dead or alive.

'I'm dead,' said the ghost.

'What's wrong that you are like this?'

'I'll be like this forever until I marry the girl I promised to marry in this world,' said the ghost. 'I have been dead for seven years and have been going about like this ever since. I was engaged to a girl before I died but I broke my promise to her and went with another girl. The first girl died of a broken heart, and I died before I could marry the other one. I'll be going round like this forever unless I get someone from this world to stand sponsor for me at my marriage in the next world. Will you do that?'

'I will!'

The ghost left him and it wasn't long before a kind of sleep came over the young man beside the fence. He awoke to find himself at the edge of a cliff. He saw an island in the sea in front of him. Sleep came over him again and when he awoke he found himself on the island. He stood up and remembered his promise to stand sponsor at a wedding. He saw a chapel some distance away and he went towards it. He went in and sat on one of the seats. It wasn't long until a priest passed by him up along the chapel, and then he saw the white ghost following, with a girl at the other side. They didn't stop till they reached the altar. The priest went up on the altar, and the ghost and the girl went on their knees. The priest called out:

'Come up here, living man, and stand sponsor for these!'

He got up from the seat and went to the altar. The priest married them and then took them into a small room. The priest wrote down in a book that the pair were married, and the young man had to write with the pen that he had been sponsor.

'Now,' said the priest to the young man, 'when you go home, you must go to the parish priest and tell him that I have married such a couple in the other world. He won't believe you, but he will get it in his book!'

'I'm very thankful to you,' said the ghost. 'This is the girl I was to marry first, but we died. Your father knew this girl well.'

They left him. Sleep came over him once more, and he awoke at the foot of the hill where he had fallen asleep first. He stood up and went off towards the wedding-house, but it was almost over. He danced a little and took a drink and ate a bite; he was very hungry after the night. When he reached home, he told his father what had happened.

'Father,' he asked, 'was there a couple like that here who died?'

'There was. I knew them well.'

'I must go to the parish priest today to tell him that they are married,' said the son.

He went to the parish priest. The priest asked him what he wanted.

'This is what I want. Go to your book of marriages and see will you find the names of a certain couple in it.'

He told the priest their names.

'Don't be telling lies! It can't be true!' said the priest.

'It might be, father. I had to promise that I'd come to you to ask you to search your book for them.'

The priest got up and went to the marriage-book. He found their names there.

'You were right,' said he.

That's my story. If there's a lie in it, let it be! I heard it about fifty years ago from an old woman named Siobhán O'Sullivan, who lived in this townland. She was about fifty years old at that time.

35 *Midnight funeral from America*

Here's a story that I'm going to tell you now, and I promise you that there's no lie in it!

The man to whom this happened was from Connemara, from a place called Garumna. He emigrated to America, not too long ago at all. He had been there four or five years, and one night he went out to visit some Irish people who were living near him. He spent a good piece of the night with them, and then said that it was time for him to return to his lodgings.

When he left them, he was walking along the street and at a corner he saw a very large funeral coming towards him, carrying a coffin on their shoulders. He had heard it always said in Ireland that one should not pass by a funeral without taking 'three steps of mercy' along with it. So he turned back and walked the three steps. As he walked, the next thing he felt was that he was carried back to Ireland, to his own place in Garumna! The graveyard was very near his old home, so when the corpse was taken in there, he ran in to his own house. The door was closed, as if the people of the house had gone out visiting. At that time it was the custom to keep a pot of boiled potatoes beside the fire for anybody who might call to the house. There was a pot near the fire, and he went over to it and took a handful of the hot potatoes. He then left the house; it was where his father and mother had lived, and where he himself was reared. He ate the potatoes and went into the graveyard.

'Now,' said he, 'this is where my father is buried here in Garumna. Isn't it strange what's happening to me tonight!'

He decided to visit his father's grave. There was a stone at its head, with his father's name and the date of his death. He knelt down and offered a Pater and Creed for his soul. He had a knife in his own pocket, with his name on it. He pulled out the knife, opened the blade and stuck it down beside the headstone where his father's head lay. He then went to where the corpse was being buried, and that was a hard job. When it was done, the people at the funeral left and he followed them. In less than an hour and a half or two hours at most from the time he had left America, he was back again at the place where he had met the funeral! The people of the funeral scattered, and he went off to the house where he was lodging. His great wonder was how far he had travelled during the night and all he had seen and done!

He went to work next day, and he found the day long till he came to his lodgings in the evening. He wrote a letter home to Ireland, giving his family the date of the day that he had met the funeral and gone to Ireland with it. He asked them had they been surprised when they came home that night that some potatoes had been taken out of the pot.

'Ye may not believe me, but it was I who was in the house that night and took the potatoes! And after that I went with a funeral that was burying a corpse in the graveyard, and I went to my father's

grave and said a Pater and Creed for his soul. When I had done that,
I put my hand in my pocket and took out a knife which had my
name and surname on it. Go to the grave, and ye will find the knife
standing beside the headstone over my father, if I'm not telling a lie!
Write back to me and tell me is my story true or not!'

Very well. They received the letter. When they came home on the
night he mentioned, everyone in the house had been surprised that
some of the potatoes were missing. They had no notion, under the
God of Graces, who took them. They went to the graveyard where
their father's grave was, and found the knife with his name and
surname on it stuck down beside the headstone. And he over in
America!

I heard that story, and there's no lie in it. 'Tisn't long since it
happened. The man was from Garumna. The dear blessing of God
and of the Church on the souls of the dead, and may ourselves and
all who are present be seventeen hundred thousand times better off,
a year from tonight, and Amen!

> Midnight funerals of a supernatural nature form the theme of many
> Irish legends. It is clear from reading or hearing them that such
> funerals may have either of two origins: (a) they are the return to
> this world for burial of humans who have died after abduction into
> fairyland; or (b) they describe the return for burial in the family
> graveyard in Ireland of Irish exiles who have died in foreign lands,
> mainly in the United States of America.

36 The San Francisco earthquake

There was a man who emigrated from the parish of Ventry to
America, and he never stopped till he made off to San Francisco. He
settled in there and was working like everybody else.

One night when he was lying in bed, tired after the day's work,
I suppose, he fell asleep. It wasn't long until he heard a voice calling
him to get up quickly. He didn't make any move the first time, but
the voice called more loudly a second time and ordered him to leave
the house immediately. He was drowsing away in the bed, moving
from one side to the other, but he didn't get up. Then a blow was

struck against the window, and he was warned to delay no longer or it would be worse for himself.

He pulled on his clothes and went out on to the street. There he met a man, and they both walked out of the city. The stranger took him so far out that he was tired from walking, and then told him to remain there.

' 'Tis a long journey I have made from the graveyard in Ventry to save you!' said the stranger.

That night the earthquake happened, and the house in which he had been sleeping was levelled to the ground.

The earthquake in question in this legend occurred in San Francisco in California in 1906. It is evident from the story that the nocturnal visitor was a dead relative or friend who had come from the graveyard in Ventry, County Kerry, to warn the exile of the impending danger.

37 The dead man's debt

A man from this district was on his way to Galway long ago and he took the road southwards by the shore. He then continued east to a place called Clynagh. There was a house there that sold poteen, and he went in to call a drink. He called for a pint of it and drank it. I don't know who was with him, but he pulled out his money to pay for the poteen. The woman of the house had no change. He said that he would pay her on his way back home. He went on to Galway then and did his business there.

He was able to take a lift home in a boat. He thought that the walk back to the poteen shop would be too long when he could go home by boat, so he went by boat. That's the year the cholera was in Galway, and I think this man had taken the cholera too. He died in the boat as it was passing Slyne Head. His body was taken home, and he was buried.

Long years went by, and there was a neighbour of his in America. One day when this neighbour was walking along a street in a place called Pittsburgh, he met the dead man.

'Don't be afraid!' said the dead man. 'You're in no danger. Have courage! The reason I have come so far to you is that I owe a woman in Clynagh some money for drink. When I went to pay her, she had

no change. I told her that I would pay her on my way home. I got
a lift home in a boat and took it, as I thought I shouldn't miss my
chance because of the price of the drink. The cholera was in Galway
at the time, and I took it, and I died as I was passing Slyne Head.
I have been going around ever since and I can't go to Heaven until
I pay that debt. The woman has never forgiven me for it, and if the
debt isn't cleared, I can't get into Heaven.'

'Why haven't you spoken to someone of your own relatives? That
would be more fit than coming to me.'

'I often intended to speak to some of them,' said the dead man,
'but the first thing they would do is to draw a knife to banish me,
so I couldn't speak to them. That same woman who sold me the
drink in Ireland is over here now, and if I could clear my debt with
her, I could get into Heaven.'

'If I paid the debt now, would it be as good as if one of your own
people did it?'

'It wouldn't matter who paid it, so long as it is paid.'

'Will you come with me now down to the public house of that
woman, to see if we can settle the matter?'

'I will.'

They went down to the house and entered. The Connemara man
called for a drink and drank it. He called again and did the same. He
then asked the woman who owned the bar had she known such a
man in Ireland. She said that she had.

'Can you remember if he ever called for a drink that he didn't pay
for?'

'I can. One time he was going to Galway; he called for a pint of
poteen and he never paid for it.'

'He didn't get a chance of paying for it. If he had, he'd pay.'

'You'd imagine that some of his relatives would pay for it after he
died,' said the woman.

'They hardly knew about it,' said he. 'You should forgive him the
debt.'

'I won't. And may God not forgive him until I get my money!'

'If I paid you now on his behalf, would you forgive him?'

'I would. It doesn't matter to me who pays it. I'll forgive him.'

'How much is it?' he asked.

She mentioned the sum, and he paid her.

'Forgive him now,' said he.

'I forgive him, and may God forgive him!' said she.

'Goodbye now,' said the ghost, and he went out through the door.

The dead were supposed to return to this world for several reasons. In the present case, the dead man could not rest until a debt which he had contracted had been paid. As the woman to whom he owed the money had emigrated to Pittsburgh in the United States, it was only natural that the debtor would ask his neighbour, who had also emigrated to that city, to help him by having the debt cleared.

38 The wave of Tóime

They say that Tonn Tóime becomes bared of water every seventh year. People used to be watching in the hope of seeing that wonder. The fairies used to have a magic cloak laid over the beautiful place when it was dry.

At last a man named Shea got a chance of seeing it. He rode out to it on his horse to take the cloak. The fairies were asleep, so he came on them unawares. He snatched the cloak, placed it behind him on the horse and rode back as quickly as he could. If he could take the cloak safely to high water mark, the magic land would remain dry forever. He had almost succeeded when the fairies awoke and guessed what was happening. The wave of Tóime rose up in anger. When Shea was within a fathom of the high water mark, the wave swept off the portion of the horse back of the saddle. Shea escaped, but the fairies kept the cloak.

They say that ever since that there is danger in the sea for anyone named Shea, especially if they go near Tonn Tóime.

In Irish tradition, there were three waves of a supernatural character off the coast: Tonn Tóime, in the present legend, in Dingle Bay, County Kerry; Tonn Chlíona, off the south coast of County Cork; and Tonn Ruairí, off the northern Irish coast. They were said to be associated with supernatural beings or fairies who lived beneath them.

39 *The cold iron spurs*

Long ago there was a man living west in a place called Errismore. He
was a young, hearty, strong fellow at first, but then he began to
decline greatly. Over a whole year, some kind of horse would come
around to the house every night and would call to the man by his
christian name and surname to come out. No matter whether he was
asleep or awake, he would have to get up and ride on the horse all
over Ireland, it seemed to him. He would be left back again next
morning. Time passed, and he was wasting away, so that, by the end
of the year, he was merely skin and bones. Anyone who had known
him earlier wouldn't recognise him at all now.

One day he took his own horse to the forge to get him shod.
When he entered, the smith didn't recognise him, although he knew
him well before that, as he often came to the forge for the same
purpose. When the smith saw who he was, he asked him what ailed
him, he looked so close to death.

'I have no pain or sickness that makes me like this,' said he. 'Still,
I'm getting weaker and weaker.'

'What's wrong with you at all?' asked the smith.

'I'll tell you,' said the young man. 'Something comes for me every
night of the year and stops outside my door. Whether I'm asleep or
awake I have to go out and ride on this thing. He takes me all
around Ireland, I think, on his back. That's what's bringing me low.'

'You won't live long, if you keep on like that,' said the smith.
'Wait until evening and I'll make a pair of spurs for you. If they
don't save you, you'll be dead before long.'

The smith took up his hammer. He picked out a piece of iron and
laid it on the anvil, without heating it, and hammered it until he
had made a pair of spurs.

'Here they are for you now,' said he, when he had them made. 'If
the thing comes for you tonight, be wearing these spurs and don't
spare using them. Make him go twice as fast as he did before, and
you on his back.'

The young man went home when his own horse was shod, and
he took the spurs with him. After midnight, the call came from
outside. The young man had already put on the spurs, fearing that

he wouldn't have time to do so when he was called. He mounted, and didn't spare using the spurs as hard as he could stretch his legs. He was taken only half as far this night as other nights. So hard was he pressing the spurs that he believed he had made holes with them, for they were sharp, and he used both legs as well as he could. The next night the thing came outside the house again and called out.

'I'm here! I'm going out to you now,' said the young man.

'Are you wearing the sharp spikes tonight?' asked the thing outside.

'I am.'

'If you are, stay inside! 'Tis a good job that you have them, for this would have been your last night alive. You may thank the sharp spikes. Only for them, 'twould be all over for you!'

The *púca* (pooka, supernatural animal like a horse) is featured in many legends which describe how a man was taken on an eerie ride by the animal at night and was left at his home, exhausted, next morning. The present legend, which is fairly common, tells how such an animal might be overcome.

Errismore is a district in County Galway.

40 *Boy abducted by fairies*

There was a young fellow fishing from a rock west in Inishnee on a summer evening. Whatever stumble came over him, he fell down the slope of the rock and was drowned.

That same night, or towards dawn next morning, there was music and dancing in a house at Bunahown to say goodbye to a young woman from there who was leaving for America. When some people were on their way home from the dance early in the morning, they heard sounds and commotion coming towards them from Inishnee, across the bay. They listened, but they couldn't see anything in the darkness. Soon they heard the sound of oars and the noise of a boat coming ashore. They could hear people getting out on to the strand, but they couldn't see them, for the side of a hill was between them. Then they thought they could hear the crying of a young fellow, as if he were trying to break free from them. Next they heard sounds of strife and confusion, as if people were fighting one another with sticks. It looked as if some of them wanted to let the young fellow, or whoever was crying, go free, and the others were against this. The fighting went on for a long time. Then the noise died down, and they heard no more. It seemed as if the crowd had gone into the hill.

That same night, a sister of the young fellow who was drowned was working in a house in America. She never saw the people of the house except in daytime. They went out each day, and she had no idea where they went. On the morning after the boy had been drowned in Inishnee in Ireland, one of the women of the house spoke to the girl and asked her from what part of Ireland she came. She told her it was Inishnee. The woman asked her had she any brother, and she said that she had.

'I'm sorry to have to tell you that he was drowned last night,' said the woman.

The girl from Inishnee was surprised that the woman could have the news so quickly. She thought that she was joking. But in a fortnight's time she got a letter telling her that her brother was drowned. Then she knew that the woman had told her the truth. Fear came over her, and she left the house altogether and went to work somewhere else.

The young woman from Bunahown met her in America later and told her what had happened, and how, on the night her brother was drowned the people going home from the dance had heard the commotion in Bunahown, and that they thought the drowned boy was being brought from Inishnee by the fairies who had taken him.

That's a story I heard. I don't know is it true or not, but, if it is a lie, 'twasn't I who made it up! The blessing of God on the souls of the dead!

As already stated (Note 21), the fairies were regarded as being bloodless, so a large number of legends tells how they abducted humans into their fairy world to try to make good the deficiency. While the present abduction of the boy was said to have taken place in Conamara, County Galway, it is clear that the family in the United States for whom his sister was working were also fairies, who were aware of what had happened in Ireland on the previous day.

41 *Fairy hurling game : Ireland v. Scotland*

There was a man named Walsh living to the east of the lake long ago. He was married. At one time he had a good stock of cattle, but he became poor and was unable to pay the rent and rates on his land. Blake was the landlord at that time, and he came and took away most of his cattle in lieu of what was due. Walsh was left with only one little beast. One foggy night came and the animal didn't come home. His wife told him to go out to search for it on the mountainside.

'I won't,' said he. ''Tis all the same now ! My cattle are gone.'

'Oh, God is good !' said his wife. 'That little animal might bring you up again !'

So out he went, and he hadn't walked far when he saw the finest man he had ever seen coming towards him.

'God to you, Seán Walsh !' said the stranger.

'God and Mary to you !' said Seán.

'Well, Seán, I have come to you now for I need your help.'

'I can't do anything just now,' said Seán. 'I'm looking for an animal of mine that's missing.'

'Your animal is safe at home now, Seán,' said the stranger. 'Come along with me !'

They walked on for a good while.

'Do you know who I am, Seán ?' said the stranger. 'No ? Well, I'm the leader of the fairy host of Connacht. Ourselves and the fairy host of Scotland are playing a hurling game against each other tonight, and if the fairy host of Scotland win, they will take all of the harvest of Ireland. If we win, the harvest will be ours.'

'I'll go with you, so,' said Seán.

'I have picked you out of all the men of Ireland for this game, Seán,' said the stranger. 'The Scots have a very good hurler to help them. He's a smith who has only one eye, and he's very strong. When the ball will be thrown up into the air at the start, if the Scot knocks you down, you'll be dead within a year, but if you knock him down, he'll die within a year.'

Very well. The Irish fairies wore green caps and the Scots red.

When the ball was thrown into the air, Seán Walsh lifted his hurley and struck the Scot above the ear. The smith fell. Seán raised the ball with his hurley and ran ahead with it, knocking down the Scots everywhere, as a storm would level hay-wisps. The havoc he caused was terrifying. When the Irish fairy host had won the game, the Connacht leader approached Seán again.

'You have done great work, Seán,' said he. 'Here is a stallion for you now. Catch his head-stall and hold him here until he whinnies three times. He will look as if he were going to eat you. Let him go loose then and watch what happens.'

Seán held on to the stallion's head-stall until he had whinnied three tmes, fearful that he would devour him. He then let the stallion go free. The fairy host from Scotland had another stallion. The two animals attacked each other. It was fearful to watch them fighting. At last the Irish stallion killed the other. The Connacht leader handed a scythe to Seán.

'Take this scythe now,' said he, 'and wield it as hard as you can against the wind.'

Seán took hold of the scythe and drew it as hard as he could against the wind for a long time. Then the Connacht leader approached him again.

'You have done wonders, Walsh !' said he. 'We have won the day ! If you could only see all that you have done, it would terrify you.'

'What I have done is small use to me when I can't see it,' said Seán.

The fairy man pulled a wisp of long grass and wound it into a ring.

'Put that to your eye, Seán,' said he. 'Look through it and see what you have done.'

When Seán put it against his eye, he could see the height of the hills and the speckling of the glens of people whom he had killed.

'You see all those you have killed, Walsh ?' asked the fairy.

'I do.'

'Take the ring from your eye now, or you will never be able to leave this place on account of the many you have killed. Here is a letter for you now ! Take it home to Blake and tell him you got it from me.

Very well. Seán bade him goodbye, took the letter and went to

Blake's house. He told a servant who came out that he wished to see Blake, he had a letter for him.

'I'll take the letter in to him,' said the servant.

He did.

'Where's the man that brought this letter?' asked Blake. 'Bring him to me.'

He was led into Blake.

'From whom did you get this letter.' says Blake.

'I got it from the finest man I have ever seen.'

'It looks very like the writing of a son of mine who died long years ago.'

'The man is your son, all right,' said Seán.

'How does he look?' asked Blake.

'Better than he did for many a day. He's the finest man I ever laid eyes on. He is the leader of the fairy host of Connacht since Finnvara died. And he says that you must return to me my two cows and let me have my piece of land rent-free – that's in his letter to you!'

Blake gave Seán back his two cows and let him have the land free for ever more. They say that Walsh died a few years after that, and that the fairy host was heard for a mile around Galway and Oughterard at night shouting for Walsh. That's a true story, I'm certain of that!

Irish fairy lore tells us that, in many respects, the fairies live more or less as human beings do in this world : they eat and drink, plant crops, own animals, quarrel among themselves, play music, sing, dance and enjoy themselves by riding about. The game of hurling seems to have been popular with them, and either team of players was anxious to have the aid of a human hurler, as in the present legend.

42 *Mockery of fairies punished*

Three women were coming home from Dingle long ago. It was a fine summer evening, and the sun was setting. They were crossing through the fields by the Small Strand in the parish of Lispole. As they were passing a *lios* (fairy fort), they heard the sweetest music in the world. The stopped a while to listen, but saw nobody. Then they said that they could imitate the music and dancing. One of them put her finger in her mouth to imitate the music ; the second whistled a tune, and the third danced. After an hour like that, they set out for home, thinking that they had done wonders. When they reached home, they were telling their story. The old people told them that music like that always left its mark on anyone who heard it, and especially on anyone who imitated it. The women said that it had left no mark on themselves.

But, alas, there was a mark on each of them when she got up next morning! The woman who had imitated the music had a swollen finger. The mouth of the woman who had whistled was twisted, and the woman who had danced had a huge foot!

Lispole is a village in West Kerry.

43 *The white gander*

There was a widow there one time and she lived somewhere near Dunmore. She had only one son and he was a kind of a fool. Faith, he learned to play the bag-pipes a little, all the same, but the only tune he could play was the Rógaire Dubh (Black Rogue). The young fellows in the place used to invite him to play here and there for the fun of it, and he would earn a little money in that way, for people had pity for him.

One Hallowe'en he was invited to play his pipes in a house two or three miles away. He went, of course, for he thought that there wasn't a better piper in Ireland than himself. When he was returning home late that night, he sat down on the parapet of a small bridge along the road, took up his pipes and started to play. Before long he saw the Pooka behind him, with his pair of long horns. The Pooka jabbed his backside with his horns and threw him on to the road.

'Bad cess to you!' said the piper. 'Why did you do that to me? All I have is a little tenpenny piece to buy snuff for my mother with.'

'Never mind your mother or her snuff!' said the Pooka. 'Play the tune of the White Gander for me.'

'That's a tune that I can't play,' said the piper.

'I'll teach it to you,' said the Pooka.

The Pooka gave him another jab with his horns and lifted him up on to the parapet of the bridge where he had been before.

'Now will you play it ?' asked the Pooka.

The piper took hold of his pipes again and began to play what he thought was the finest music he had ever knocked out of the pipes.

'You'll do what I need,' said the Pooka. 'The fairy host sent me out tonight to search for a musician. You'll have to come with me to the house of the fairy woman on the top of Croagh Patrick and play music for them until morning.'

'That's good stroke of luck for me,' said the piper. 'When I was at Confession this year, Father Doncha put a penance on me that I'd have to make a pilgrimage to Croagh Patrick on account of stealing a white gander from him. 'Twill be easier for me to go there along with you than any other way !'

'I promise you that you'll be well paid for your night's music,' said the Pooka.

The Pooka then put his horns under the piper and lifted him on to his back. Off he went faster than the wind, through bogs and mountains and fields, through rough land and smooth land, through woods and scrub and bushes and briars, and past harbours. The devil a finer ride had the piper ever got before than he did that night ! It didn't take them long to reach the top of Croagh Patrick. They were barely there when the Pooka put his horns under a rock that was there and threw it aside to show a fine, wide opening beneath it. The pair of them went in and came to a fine door. The Pooka struck it with one of his horns and opened it. In they went to a beautiful room with grand furniture. About a hundred old women were seated at a large table in the middle of the floor. They all stood up and had a thousand welcomes for the Pooka.

'Who is this that's with you ?' they all asked together.

'He's the finest piper in Ireland. I met him and brought him here to ye tonight.'

'You're my thousand loves !' said one of them. 'We haven't had a dance as long as we can remember, for want of a musician.'

They joyfully took hold of the piper and carried him around the big room, and gave him the finest drink of brandy that he had ever got in his life. Then one of the old women tapped with her foot against the bottom of the wall, and a large door opened there. What came out through the door but the white gander he had stolen from the priest the previous summer ! One of the old women ordered the gander to remove the table, as they wanted to dance. When the poor gander had done that, he was ordered to bring in the music chair for the piper. When the chair was brought in, the piper sat on it, and the gander pricked him on the backside.

'You'll play the tune I'll make for you, you black rogue !' said the gander.

The gander started to scream and squawk, and the piper began to play. The devil such fine music as he knocked out of the pipes nobody had ever heard before ! All the old women went out dancing, and you may call it fine dancing ! When they were tired, the gander pricked a hole in the bag of the pipes and the music stopped. At the end of the dance, all the old women had become young girls !

'Only for the gander pricking the hole in your bag,' said one of them to the piper, 'you'd keep on playing till we'd all draw our last breath !'

They couldn't stop dancing while the music went on. They were all very grateful to the piper, and they ordered the gander to get another set of pipes for him quickly. The gander did this, and all the girls gave the piper a golden guinea each for the night's music. They also gave him the gift of being the best piper in Ireland. He said goodbye to them then, and the Pooka came and took him on his back.

'I promised you that you'd be well paid for the night,' said the Pooka, 'and now you have three gifts. You have sense and gold and the gift of music from this night on.'

Off they went back the way they had come until they reached the little bridge near Dunmore. They were there just as the cock was crowing in the morning. The Pooka said goodbye to him then, and the piper went home to his mother. They lived in love and comfort from that time on. They had plenty, and to spare. That's the story of the White Gander.

Reference is often to be found in songs and stories to the imposition of a pilgrimage to Croagh Patrick, a mountain in Mayo, as penance for sin. A very large pilgrimage still takes place to the mountain-top in late July or early August each year.

Names for dance-tunes, such as the Black Rogue and the White Gander, were very numerous in Ireland, the individual title having no particular significance, as a rule.

For the Pooka, see Legend No. 39.

V
Special Powers

In Irish legends one often finds mention of individuals who were said to have special powers, which were not given to the normal run of persons. The seventh son or daughter in succession, the child born with a caul or posthumously, persons with the evil eye, tongue or heart, saints, widows, the silenced priest, charm-setters, women from Ulster and others belonged to this special category. Legends about such persons are legion, and only a few can be given here.

44 *The seventh son*

My father and mother had one daughter, Máire, and seven sons :
Con, Eón, Dónal, Pádraig, Seán, Séamus and myself, Mícheál. I was
the seventh son, one after the other, and I was born on the Feast of
Saints Peter and Paul.

They say that the seventh son has a cure, and I think it is true,
for I cured evil many times. The only kind of evil I couldn't cure was
bone-evil. I don't think anybody could cure that.

I often tried to kill worms and things like that, and I could do
it any time of the day. I would put the worm on a flat stone or on
a shovel or something like that ; then I would bless myself, in the
Name of the Father and of the Son and of the Holy Ghost. I would
be fasting, and I would wet my right thumb in my mouth and draw
a circle with it around the worm and make the Sign of the Cross
over it two or three times. The worm could never leave the circle ;
it would turn belly-up and die. I haven't done it now for a very long
time ; I dropped it.

Some years ago, my brother's daughter was a servant girl in the
house of Doncha O'Shea in Clogherane. One autumn day, a fairy
wind struck the hay and swept it away from them. The wind
returned again, and this girl happened to be in its path as it blew
through the field. It struck her and went through her. A week or a
fortnight after that, her jaw grew sore and started to swell. It broke
out and the world wouldn't cure it. There was white pus coming out
through the centre of it all the time, between the jaw and the
tongue. She came to me, after trying many others, and I carried out
the cure two mornings and cured her. She's over in America now,
strong and healthy and well-off. It never troubled her since. My
mother was against my trying to cure her, as I had children of my
own, and told me not to do it. I said that I would, no matter what
happened to me. I took her out to the cow-house and made the Sign
of the Cross fervently over her. The sore had dried up by the second
morning.

They say that if you could see the fairy wind coming towards you
and were handy enough to throw a wisp of hay against it and say :
'May my harm and evil go with you !', it would not touch you.

I often tried to cure people who had some bad complaint. There was a young woman named Máire Cumba in Gurranes, and she was at the marriageable age. She had a bad score in her breast. She came to me when I was a child, and she was joking me that I would have to marry her, if I cured her. I was in bed in the room below the kitchen, and I was brought up to her. Two or three held me while I made the Sign of the Cross over her. I did that for two or three mornings and cured her.

I remember that there were two boys east in Baureeragh, near Bonane. They were relatives of mine. Their throats were breaking out from ear to ear. I was brought east to them, and spent three days there. I cured their evil. They went to America and it never troubled them since.

There's another complaint that attacks people, especially young people. Big boils break out on them and they are hard to cure. We call them *piastaí* (worms). The boil grows three or four skins before it breaks. The only cure for it is that a seventh son or a seventh daughter would make the Sign of the Cross over it. This kills the *piastaí*. I often cured people of that. It is easier to cure than evil.

I knew very well the seventh son, who gave me this account of himself and of his powers as a healer. I recorded many legends of the supernatural, as well as lore about birds and animals, from him. He died on 4 January 1938.

The places mentioned in the story are in the Parish of Tuosist, County Kerry.

45 *A widow's curse*

There was a widow woman called O'Neill, and she was carrying a can of water down the road. The landlord from the Glen was travelling east in a coach drawn by two horses, and one of his cattle which were grazing along the road had gone into the widow's field.

'Mary,' said the landlord to her, 'I'm going to clear you out of this place as soon as I come back from Killarney. My cattle are short of grass.'

Off he went. She went down on her two knees.

'I ask God and His holy Mother that you may not return !' said she.

It was true for her. He didn't return. The sickness of death
overtook him at Gleesk, and he died.

They say that a widow's curse isn't good when she has cause for
it, and I suppose 'tis true.

Many landlords were disliked, even hated, by their tenants, especially
if they were heartless and tyrannical.
Gleesk is in the Barony of Iveragh in West Kerrry.

46 *Saint Conall's stone*

There is a townland called Cashel here in Connemara in County
Galway, and there is a holy well in it called Conall's Well. There was
a flag-stone over the well in the old days, and people would turn it
around against the sun as a curse on anyone who acted wrongly.
Each time that the curse fell, a piece would break away from the side
of the stone.

My grandfather told me that he was living near that place and that
a travelling woman came to their house late one evening. When she
entered she sat near the door. She was a stranger to them, so they
invited her to draw up to the fire, but she said that she wasn't cold.
They then said that, even though she mightn't be cold, she might
be tired after a long journey. She said that she was tired, but had to
hurry on. She asked them where was Conall's Well. They told her
it wasn't far away, only a couple of hundred yards. The question
didn't appear strange to them at all. She asked them to show her the
well, and they went out and did so and returned to the house. She
went on to the well. They took no great notice of anything or
suspected her of any evil intention.

She was only about a half-hour at the well when such storm and
gale and rain came that they feared every house and cow-house in the
townland would be levelled to the ground. What had brought her
to the well was to turn the flag-stone against a man who had
wronged her daughter and married another woman. She wanted
Saint Conall to settle matters. The man and his brother and father
were at sea in a boat and they were drowned at that time, along with
many others.

When my own grandfather heard the gale and the bad weather, he took fright. He went to the well along with two other men from the townland, and they took the flag-stone and sank it down into a boghole, where nobody would ever find it to harm anyone again. From that day to this, the stone hasn't been turned, because no one could find it in the bog, which is near the well at Cashelard.

That's my story, as I heard it myself from my grandfather. The dear blessing of God and of the Church on the souls of the dead, and may we be better a year from tonight !

The practice of pronouncing a curse on somebody, while turning a stone or anvil, in the case of a smith, anti-sunwise, is often mentioned in Irish oral tradtion.

The places mentioned in the legend are in West Galway. Holy wells were centres for prayers and pilgrimages.

47 Ulster woman's magic

A hag from Ulster and her daughter used to travel around this country long ago, and one night they got lodgings in a house west in Errismore. The young people of the place came in to see the strangers. A young fellow among them started to say some unseemly things to the daughter, and the mother didn't like that and became angry.

It was the summer fishing season. The following day was fine, and the men, old and young, went out fishing. When they were at sea, the Ulster hag took a pot, filled it with water and hung it on the fire until it boiled. She put the stick of the kneading-trough into the boiling water and went on her knees. She ordered her daughter to keep looking into the pot. According as the boiling water rose high in the pot, the sea began to foam and rise in the same way. As the boiling water overflowed into a cup that she had, the sea poured into the boats. This continued until the flowing cup sank in the pot.

'The cup is sunk!' said the daughter.

'If it is,' said the Ulster hag, 'the boats are sunk too. Let us leave here!'

Off they went. She drowned hundreds that day. You have often heard that a shipful of people might be drowned because of one person. But the fellow whom she wanted to take revenge on wasn't drowned at all, nor were those who were in the boat with him. They had a rowing-boat, which had a sprig of rowan on board, and that prevented the hag from sinking the boat. They all came safe to shore.

That story is as true as any you heard since you were baptised. The dear blessing of God on the souls of the dead, and long life to the Ediphone!

In many countries, magical powers were generally supposed to belong to those who lived in the north. In Ireland, many women who travelled around in the south, were referred to as *mná Ultacha* (Ulster women, 'oultachs') and were credited with unusual powers of healing, knowledge and magic. For a tale similar to the present one, see O'Sullivan, *Folktales of Ireland,* No. 42, 226-7.

The rowan (mountain ash) tree was credited with great protective powers in Irish folk belief.

48 *Three evil wives punished*

There was a ship's captain there long ago; he had a mate and a second mate on the ship. They were going to put to sea, and the three of them got married the same day. They put the three wives to live in the same house and got ready to sail.

Before they left port, the captain found that he had forgotten something and he sent the cabin-boy to the house to fetch it. The boy found the door of the house closed and locked. He could hear talk inside and he listened. What was it but the three wives had a tub of water in the middle of the floor, and a basin floating on top! They carried out some kind of magic which ruffled the water and almost sank the basin. After a time, the basin sank to the bottom of the tub.

'We'll do the job!' said one of the women.

'Indeed we will!' said the second wife.

'If they knew how to save themselves, they'd kill us,' said the third. 'If they stuck a knife into the bow of the ship, they could save themselves and we'd be dead!'

The boy was listening to them all the time, and he made up his mind to do what they said. He knocked at the door, and was let in. When he got the message, he returned to the ship. The vessel left harbour and after a few days' sailing, the sea rose mountains high in a storm, so that the crew had to fold the sails altogether. But it was no use; the sea was doing what it wished with them, so that the ship was almost sunk. When this had gone too far, the boy ran forward to the bow and stuck his knife into one side of it. The sea grew calm immediately, and there wasn't a puff of wind. The captain asked the boy what he had done and then he told him the whole story.

The captain turned his ship about and headed for the harbour again. They went ashore, and the captain made off the house. The door was locked and he couldn't get in. He broke down the door. And there were the three wives in the middle of the floor with the tub of water. Their heads were under the water and they were drowned. A knife was stuck into the body of each.

The magical technique used by the three wives in this legend resembles that mentioned in Legend No. 47. The women in both cases hoped to produce a storm by sympathetic magic.

49 *Earwig in sickle*

There was a man named Sean Burke from this place, and he used to go to the same place, Kilkenny, every year, saving the harvest and digging potatoes. He spent fourteen years like that, and during all that time he lodged with the same old man and his wife every year. This man and Burke worked for the same farmer.

The grain crop used to be planted in ridges, and two reapers worked at each ridge. Burke and the old man always reaped together. The farmer had twelve men in all, reaping in pairs. The work came easy to Burke, for the old man reaped most of each ridge. Burke had never met a better reaper before. When he went to Kilkenny for the fifteenth year, he was told that the old man had died a year before. The old widow was alone.

'Oh,' says she, 'your old comrade died since you were here last year. He's gone!'

Burke was very sad at the news, and he began to tell her how sorry he was after spending so many harvests working together.

'He spoke about you two days before he died,' said she, 'and he ordered me to give you the old sickle that he had every year, if you came again. I have it here for you, if you'll take it.'

'I will gladly,' said Burke.

Well, he lodged with her again, as he did every other year. Next day he went to the same farmer and was hired. He started to reap with another man and took with him his own sickle and the one that the old man had willed for him. When they started work in the morning, Burke took up the old man's sickle to see was it any use. It didn't look like a sickle at all; it was more like a knife, with no teeth at all. He started to reap with it, and it seemed to him that the old sickle was able to reap of its own accord, without any help from himself. His comrade had very little to do, as Burke was reaping most of the ridge.

When they had reaped the whole ridge to the end of the field, Burke pretended to find fault with the way the handle was fixed on the sickle. He went over to the fence, struck the handle a few taps with a stone and loosened it. When he pulled off the handle, what ran out from the hole in it but a big black earwig! He didn't know, live or dead, how it had got in there. Wasn't it a strange thing! He fixed the handle back on to the sickle again, as he liked it to be, and the two of them went to the other end of the field. Himself and his comrade started to reap again. But the old sickle was useless and couldn't cut anything. Burke had a notion that it was the earwig that had made the old sickle so powerful up to then.

This legend is found very commonly in Irish oral tradition. The earwig *(dara daol)* was regarded as evil, since a legend tells how it spied on Our Saviour when He was fleeing from His enemies, and should be killed at sight.

50 *Four-leafed shamrock*

There was a Claddagh man, and he had a quarter-acre of potatoes planted a mile and a half to the east of Galway. The Burkes owned the land. He had an ass and a small milch cow. He went to his patch of land one day, with a rope and sickle, to cut some hay from a fence there for the little ass and cow. He cut it and took it on his back. When he was going home by the side of the Green in Galway, what did he see coming towards him but a large crowd of people! Out in front of them was a cock, and everyone in Galway was coming to see him and to follow him. Some of the man's own neighbours were there too, and he stopped when he met them. He couldn't see what was causing them all the wonder.

'Where are ye going? Or what are ye all wondering at?' he asked a couple of them.

'Did you ever see such a wonderful thing?' asked one of them.

'What wonder?'

'Do you see the huge baulk of wood that the cock is pulling?' asked the neighbour.

'What baulk is he pulling?' asked the Claddagh man. 'That's only a wisp of straw!'

'Whist!' said the others. 'Don't you see the big baulk that he has pulled down from the dockside?'

'Indeed, he hasn't! All that he's pulling is a wisp of straw!' said the Claddagh man.

Who should hear him saying this but the circus-man!

'Whisper, would you sell that bundle of hay to me?' says he to the Claddagh man.

The Claddagh man had a notion that the *seamair Mhuire* (four-leafed shamrock) was in the bundle on his back.

'Oh, I want the bundle myself!' said he.

'I need it very badly,' said the circus-man. 'How much do you want for it? I'll give you all you ask, for I want it for my horses.'

He offered the Claddagh man seven times the value of the hay, and the money enticed him. The circus-man paid him and took the bundle from him. And the Claddagh man could swear, when he parted with the bundle, that it was a baulk of wood the cock was pulling, as all the people were saying!

This legend refers to County Galway and tells of the special powers attributed to the four-leafed shamrock (clover). For a version of the legend from Kerry, see O'Sullivan, *Folktales of Ireland,* No. 41, and accompanying bibliography.

51 *Bewitched cow*

I have a story, and it is a true one, about a boy who bewitched a cow belonging to his own father. He was two years older than I. His name was Andy Connell.

We were down on the strand searching for eels as fishing-bait, and on our way back home we passed through the herd of cows. He started to praise one of the cows, and, if he did, it wasn't long until she started to shiver and she fell down in the field, with her head stretched out from her.

'You have bewitched the cow, Andy!' I said.

He became frightened.

'Now, spit on her,' said I, 'and say "God's blessing on her!"' '

He spat on her three times, and she rose up in front of us as well as she had ever been. She began to graze again.

In magic, harm might be caused to others in any of three ways: (*a*) by the evil eye (which some persons might unwittingly possess), (*b*) by the evil tongue (curse), or (*c*) by the evil heart (jealousy). The evil result could be avoided or rectified by the utterance of a prayer ('God bless it!') or by the application of spittle, as in the present instance.

52 *Rats cut their throats*

Long years ago a big ship came in to Waterford Quay with a cargo of yellow meal. There were hundreds of tons of it in the hold and everywhere else, so that it took six long months to empty it out.

Glory be to God! Don't talk about money! That's the time a man could earn money! And a shilling would go seven times as far then as it would go now! Two brown pennies for a pint of beer, and it strong enough for a hen to walk on it! 'Twas it would put strength into a man! It was no trouble for us that time to carry a sack of yellow meal across the quay on our shoulders.

But talking of this big ship, it was full of rats. They gathered into it from the cellars and drains of the city. It was the smell of the yellow meal that drew them. The captain of the ship was afraid to put to sea, as she might scnk on account of being rent and torn by the devils of rats. They are a misfortunate tribe, wherever they are! That was good and it wasn't bad! The captain issued a proclamation in every newspaper in Ireland, saying that he would give so much money to anyone who would come and banish the rats. Time passed, until there were only two or three days left before he would have to put to sea. He would have to pay heavy tax if he remained in port for any time over what was agreed in the bargain he had made with the harbour commissioners. He was sad and disheartened, poor man.

On the day before he would have to sail, a man came across the quay. To look at, you wouldn't think him worth any more than an old ten of clubs! He came aboard the ship.

'I want to have a word with you,' said he to the captain. 'I saw a notice in a paper that you were tormented by rats, and that you'd give so much money to whoever would get rid of them.'

'That's just how things are,' said the captain. 'And to make matters worse, I'll be sailing on tomorrow's tide.'

No one knew who this stranger was. All he did was to draw the stump of an old razor out of his pocket, and stick it down through one of the planks of the deck, with the edge upwards. He then pulled out a book and started to read it. He hadn't much of it read before every one of the rats, small and big, old and young, speckled and white and yellow, came up the gangway. Each of them went over to the razor and cut his throat against it. All there was soon was a flood of blood on the deck! The stranger took his wages and left the ship.

This tale was recorded from memory by Seán Ó Dúnaí, a teacher of Irish in County Waterford.

Rats were a pest in olden times, and the services of poets and persons who knew the requisite charm were often called upon to banish them. For a version of this legend from County Galway, see O'Sullivan, *Folktales of Ireland,* No. 39, and accompanying note.

VI
Religious Legends

Many apocryphal legends about Our Saviour, the Virgin Mary and the saints are to be found in Irish oral tradition. Many of them have a deep religious feeling, and it is probable that some, at least, of them were used by preachers as *exempla*. In general, they have a medieval flavour.

53 *The bundle of straw*

There were two old sisters living here long ago in a townland called Corveen. An old brother named Paddy lived along with them. The sisters were very religious, but Paddy had no faith at all, or any regard for God or man. The sisters used to go to Mass every Sunday, and Paddy used to scold them when they left the house. When they were setting out for the church one fine Sunday in autumn, he threatened to kill them if they didn't stay at home to help him to save the harvest. One of the sisters was foolish enough to stay behind, but the other said that she wouldn't, even if he broke every stick in the house! Off she went, and the other sister stayed to help Paddy with the harvest.

That was that! Time passed, and the years went by until Paddy died. When he was on his death-bed, the sisters did all they could to get the priest to him, but he wouldn't listen to them. He died without the priest. He was waked and buried. The sisters felt his death keenly, and one of them died soon afterwards. The other was alone then, without anybody to help her.

At that time the people of this district had a custom, which is gone now. When a body was buried, they would put the straw of the bed on which the person had died in a special place, and the relatives would go once a day or so to pray for the soul of the dead person at the place where the straw was stored. One day the sister, who was still alive, went with some other women to pray where the dead sister's straw was. Didn't she make a mistake and pray instead where Paddy's straw was kept! It wasn't long before she noticed the other bundle of straw moving, and the voice of the dead sister spoke to her. It told her to come over to her bundle of straw; that it was useless to pray where she was, as Paddy was damned! She should pray for her, and she would have been damned also only for the day she had gone to Mass in spite of Paddy; it was the Mass she had fervently attended that day that had saved her; the other Masses had not helped her at all!

'But I'm not in Heaven yet!' said the voice. 'That's why I'm here today to tell you my trouble. When I was a young girl, growing up, Paddy used to be very severe on me. He was too lazy himself to get up in the morning to feed the cattle, and I would have to do it,

summer and winter, no matter how the weather was. One morning
he sent me out to get some straw for the cattle. There was a cover
of snow on the ground, and I was barefoot. On my way to where
our own fodder was, another man had a rick of straw, and I said to
myself that it would be no harm to take some of his, as the morning
was cold. I stole a bundle of it, and from that day to this, I never
confessed to that man what I had done. Nor did I pay him either,
and now I can't get into Heaven ever until I pay him, or someone
else does so on my behalf.'

'Well, I'll pay him,' said the sister, 'as soon as I go home.'

She went home, took a bundle of straw to the man and told him
the whole story.

'Well,' said the man, 'if that kept your sister out of Heaven, I'll
never see the face of God, for I have stolen, since I was born, as
much as would send half of the congregation to Hell!'

The custom of storing the straw of a death-bed in a particular place,
as recounted here from Donegal, is, to my mind, rare in Ireland now;
it may, of course, have been practised more widely in former times.
Legends of unrest for the dead, either because of the breaking of the
Sabbath or of some theft, are very common in Ireland.

54 Dead mother and children come for dying father

There was a man there long ago and he had three sons. Two of them
died young, but the third grew up to be a fine, big man, and he
worked at home. At last his father and mother died, and he was left
alone. He was lonely for a long time. One night he went out for a
walk, and it wasn't long till he met his mother – she had been dead
for a while at this time.

'Is it here you are, in the Name of God?' said he to her. 'I have
been praying for you every day since you left this world.'

'The two sons that I had have done me more good than all the
prayers you ever said!' said the mother.

'If that's the way things are, I won't pray any more for you,' said he.

He turned back home and pondered for a long time on what he should do. Great fear came over him. He made up his mind that he would leave home and travel like a beggar-man. He rose early next morning, got ready for the road and set out. He was well-educated for he had spent some time learning in a college. He travelled on and on until he came to a house at the roadside. He went in, and the people of the house had a great welcome for him. There were the father and mother, two sons and a daughter. A master was teaching the girl, and when he left the house that night, the traveller started to teach her. The people of the house noticed that he was far better than the master. They gave him lodgings for the night, and when he was getting ready to leave next morning, they asked him to stay with them altogether.

He stayed and taught the daughter for a long time. At the end, she fell in love with him so much that she took to her bed with her heart broken. He wanted to leave the house, but they said that they'd kill him unless he married the girl. He had to marry her and they lived with her family. At last a baby was born to the young couple, but it died after being baptised. The mother was very sad, but the young father shed no tear at all. After a time, another baby was born, and the same thing happened. It died and was buried. Next day the two sons spoke to their father.

'What kind of a man is that you have brought into this house?' they asked.

'How is that?' said the father.

'We'll tell you. He hasn't shed a tear for his two children that died.'

'What's the harm in that?' asked the father. 'Let him do as he wishes.'

'We won't!' said the sons. 'If it happens again, we'll shoot him!'

Very well! The same thing happened when the next baby was born. It died, and the father shed no tear. Sunday came a few days later, and the two sons got ready early and took their guns with them, so that they could meet the other man on his way to Mass and kill him. He left the house to go to Mass a good while later, and, as if he knew that the pair were looking for him, he took a short-cut to the church. That saved his life. When he returned from Mass, the pair who had left earlier in the morning were already at home.

'Ye went off very early this morning,' said he to them, 'still I didn't see ye at Mass.'

'Indeed, you didn't!' said they. 'It wasn't to Mass we went this morning, but to shoot you! You can be thankful that you took the short-cut, or you'd be dead!'

'If that's the way things are, I won't stay here a day longer!'

He went back to his old home. The house was lonely, for it had been empty for many a day; still he settled down there again. His wife was very lonely after him, and she was so sad that she became ill and had to stay in bed. She spent a good while that way, and at long last she died, poor woman, of a broken heart. Then one night her husband went to bed in his own room. Later in the night, he heard the sweetest music anyone had ever listened to. What was it but his dead wife and her three dead children who had come for him! He lay back again in bed, poor man, and he died. Late next day, a neighbour called at the house, but he saw nobody there. When he went in, he found the man dead in his room. They say that his wife and children had come for him, to take him up to Heaven.

There are other legends in Ireland which tell of the near-despair which comes over a man on hearing that his prayers have been unheard by God. The seeming indifference of the parent to the death of his children is illustrated, as already referred to, by No. 7 in the present volume.

55 *Value of a Pater and a Creed*

Long ago we had landlords here, and they were very severe on the poor tenants. They picked rent from them twice a year, and those who were demanding very high rents were the worst of all. They would take away the cow and the calf, if the money wasn't there to give them. And where was the money? It wasn't there at all. There was one poor old man, with his family, and he had been picked clean by the tyrant of a landlord, so that he had nothing at all left.

'Now,' said he to the landlord, 'I have nothing to give you. You have already taken the cow and the calf, the sheep and the lamb. I have nothing more. But I'll say a Pater and a Creed for you each day for a year, and I'll bless you, but don't evict myself and my family.'

'How do we know the value of a Pater and a Creed for a year?' asked the tyrant.

'We'll ask the parish priest,' said the poor man.

'Very well!' said the big man. 'Then we'll know their value.'

The poor man said a Pater and a Creed every day for a year, and he said them fervently that the landlord would leave him in his house, and would be kind to him during the year and afterwards. When the year was up, the poor man went to the priest, and told him his story.

'Oh!' said the priest, 'those prayers are so valuable that I can't tell you how much they are worth. We'll ask the bishop.'

They asked the bishop, and he sent back a paper by the messenger: 'The prayers are so valuable that I am unable to say what they are worth, but I'll ask the Pope in Rome.'

The Pope wrote back, on a fine, large sheet of paper, that a Pater and a Creed fervently said by a holy person was worth a bar of gold that would reach from the earth to the top of the sky. That was their value! The bishop got the letter and sent it to the parish priest, who read it to both the landlord and the poor man.

'How can I pay you that much, Tadhg?' said the tyrant.

'I'm not asking you to pay it, master,' said poor Tadhg.

'All that I have in the world or a thousand times more wouldn't reach that amount,' said the tyrant. 'But you can have your land and your little house, and I'll build a better house for you. You may keep it until the day you die, and the same goes for your relatives. And don't die of hunger! As long as I have anything to give you, you'll get it, and well you deserve it!'

And so far as I know or can guess, that landlord wasn't as hard on his tenants afterwards, as he had been before. He grew holy and understood life better, and he realised that he had been acting unjustly previously. It was that poor old man and his Pater and Creed for a year that made him humble. Praise be to God and to the saints and apostles!

This legend has a strong medieval flavour and may well have been used in sermons as an *exemplum* in former times. The reference of a problem, first to a priest, then to a bishop, and finally to the Pope, occurs as a motif in a number of folktales.

56 *The old woman's prayer*

This old woman used to be travelling about asking for alms. The only prayer she knew was a short one, but she said it often :

'May the Father and the Son and the Holy Ghost protect me today and through the year !'

She reached a house one night and asked for lodgings until morning. She got them and went to bed in a room that was there. It was a house of robbers – three sons, who lived with their father. The father was always praying that God would show in some way the right road to his sons. The three sons made a plan that they would murder the old woman when she went to sleep. One of them went to the door of her room and peered in through the keyhole. What did he see but a guard, dressed in a white garment and carrying a gun, walking up and down beside the bed ! He told this to the two brothers. The second brother looked into the room and saw two guards there. And when the third brother looked in, he saw three ! They had been given a sign by God and they gave up robbery.

For the protective power of the single prayer of an innocent person, see also Ó Súilleabháin, *Scéalta Cráibhtheacha,* No. 81, and Herbert, *Romances,* III, 356.

57 *Child's soul in a tree*

There was a man there long ago, and he was a finished thief ! He spent all his time stealing and robbing and thieving. He wanted to take, in one way or another, anything he laid his eyes on. He had no fear of God or of eternal damnation. He wasn't worried about his soul so long as he wasn't caught in the act. He kept on like that, and getting worse he was, the older he grew.

He left his house one night and took his axe with him and never stopped until he went into the land of a neighbouring gentleman. He wanted to cut down a big tree that was growing there and take it home. It was near the dead hour of night when he came to where the tree was standing. He took off his coat, trussed up his sleeves and started to work, cutting the tree. He kept on cutting until he was as far in as the heart of the trunk. He stopped to wipe the sweat from his brow, and while he was doing so, a voice spoke in the heart of the tree, saying :

'Shame ! Shame ! What's this you are doing to a poor soul which needs only one other hour to finish its purgatory ?

Terror and trembling came over the thief. The axe fell from his hand through fright and fear.

'Who are you that's talking to me ?' he asked, when he recovered his voice. 'Are you alive or dead ?'

'I am a child,' said the voice, 'who was born at the first cock-crow. I was baptised at the second cock-crow, and I died at the third. When I went into eternity, I was told that I wasn't yet fit to go into the sight of God, glory be to Him, or into the company of the blessed in the City of Heaven. I would have to return to this world again and spend twenty-one years in purgatory here until the stain of original sin was cleansed from my soul. My purgatory was to be spent in this tree that you are cutting tonight. I had to spend seven years between the bark and the wood on the cold and windy side of the tree ; seven more years between the bark and the wood on the sunny side of the tree : and the last seven years here inside the heart of the tree. I have spent all my time of purgatory now except one hour. When the cock crows, my soul will leave this place and go up into the presence of God and the blessed. Have patience for a while now and let me finish my purgatory !'

The man threw himself on the ground and beat his breast in anguish.

'May God help a poor, unfortunate sinner like me, whose soul is covered with sins !' said he. 'What chance have I of going into the presence of God and the blessed when I leave this world, if a small, innocent baby like you, who never committed a sin, has to spend twenty-one years in purgatory in this world before catching sight of the beauty of Heaven ?'

'You have time still,' said the voice again. 'Better late than never ! It was for you and for people like you that Our Saviour was crucified on the Cross. He will forgive you, if you repent. Go off home now ! Never steal or rob again, as long as you live, and God will reward you. You will see His mansion and His wonderful powers when you go into His presence.'

The man stood up, put on his coat and took his axe home. And from that day until the day of his death, he didn't steal or thieve. He changed his way of life. He restored, as far as he could, all that he had stolen before that, and he lived in the love of God, at peace with his neighbours, afterwards.

It would be contrary to present Christian belief that an innocent child should suffer in Purgatory. The tale may have been used as an *exemplum,* however, to demonstrate the evil of theft. The confining of an evil spirit into a narrow space is common in other legends (between the froth and the water, or between the bark of a tree and the wood).

58 *'Twixt saddle and ground*

There was a man there long ago, and a long time ago it was. If I were there then, I wouldn't be there now. I'd have a new story or an old story, or maybe I'd be without any story ! This man was doing every kind of badness, and stealing and robbing. One day he was riding his horse by the side of a river. The sun shone for a moment, and the rider heard someone laughing. He drew up his horse and caught sight of a person.

'Why are you laughing ?' asked the rider.

The man who had laughed was standing in the current of the river.

'Last night a baby boy was born to my grandson, and he'll be a priest later on. The first Mass he will celebrate will release me from here.'

'How long have you been here ?' asked the rider.

'Twenty years next Easter Sunday.'

'What sins had you committed ?'

'When I was young' said the man in the river, 'I mocked and made fun of everybody and had little pity for those who were afflicted.'

'Well,' said the rider, 'I have no chance at all of saving my soul !'

He dismounted in order to take his stand in the river. And between the stirrup and the ground his sins were forgiven, as he had examined his conscience and submitted to what was in store for him.

' 'Twixt saddle and ground
Mercy he asked for, mercy found.'
Legends which tell of the hope of a soul in Purgatory that it will
be released much later on through a Mass to be said by a priest, as
yet a child or even unborn, are common in Irish oral tradtion. The
idea of a soul doing Purgatory in a river is reminiscent of the basic
motif in Type 756, 'The Three Green Twigs', Thompson, *Types*.

59 *Cian of the Golden Ears*

Cian of the Golden Ears lived to be fairly old. He was a great thief.
Nothing escaped him, without stealing it, except something that was
either too heavy or too hot! When he grew old, he became afraid
of death and of the next world, so he sent for the priest and made
his confession to him. He told him about all that he had done
during his life. He confessed that he had spent his time badly and
that he had done a great deal of thieving. When he had told the
priest everything, 'What do you think of my chances, Father?' he
asked.

'I find it hard to say,' said the priest. 'I'm afraid that you have
spent your life badly, and 'tis likely that you'll go down below! If
you get any chance of coming back after your death, I'd like very
much that you'd bring me an account of how you got on when you
went into eternity. You haven't long more in this life, I'm afraid!'

'Since you asked me that,' said Cian, 'if I have any chance at all
of coming back to tell you how I got on, I'll come, but don't blame
me if I don't!'

Within two or three weeks, the priest was saying Mass in the
chapel. There was a window behind the altar. It was a fine, sunny
Sunday, and there was a streak of sunshine coming in through the
window and shining across the chapel. All the people, except a few
late-comers, were inside. Then a fine, active-looking man came in,
carrying an overcoat on his arm and a hat in his hand. He walked
up in front of the altar. The sunbeam was coming in through the
window. The man looked about him, to see was there any seat he
could take or on which he could lay his coat and hat. He couldn't
see any vacancy, and the people were on their knees. All the man did
was to catch hold of his coat and throw it across the sunbeam. If he

did, the sunbeam supported it ! He put his hat on top of the coat and got on his knees and blessed himself.

The priest could see all that the man did, and he was filled with wonder how he was able to do it, and how the sunbeam was able to support the coat and hat. He looked towards the congregation and called to them, asking had they noticed or seen anything wonderful. Only three replied, saying that, faith, they had, and that this man wasn't of this world, but rather some holy man, to say that the sunbeam was supporting his coat and hat.

'Of course, ye know,' said the priest, 'that that's the truth. He must be a holy man to say that the sunbeam is supporting his coat and hat. I would like very much, stranger,' said he, 'if you would tell me who you are or where you come from.'

'You surely knew Cian of the Golden Ears,' said the stranger. 'You anointed him one day. You were talking to him three weeks ago, and you made him promise you solemnly that, if he had any chance in the world, he would come back to you with an account of how he got on. You are talking to Cian now.

'I am Cian of the Golden Ears,' said he,
'I have more than I need for my life ;
I never turned anyone away from my house,
And I wasn't turned away from God's house.
There is danger that you will yourself go
To where you said I would go !'

The Irish title of the main character in this legend is Cian na mBeann Óir, in which the word 'Beann' may mean either ears or horns. It is not clear how he got this name. For the inset motif F1101.1, 'Clothes hung on sunbeam', see Stith Thompson, *Motif-Index ;* also Cross, *Motif-Index.* Heavenly reward for charity is a common theme in Irish legendry.

60 *The Spanish sailor*

There was a Spaniard there long ago ; he had been born in Spain. One day he told his mother that he was going on board a ship as a sailor.

'If you are, son,' said she, 'you must pray on your rosary beads every time you have a chance, asking that you will have a priest with you when you are dying.'

He promised her that he would. He went on a ship and during his time as a sailor, he saved a lot of money, which he kept in a leather belt around his body. At last he felt that death was not far away from him, so he asked the sailors on the ship to land him at the back of the mountains above at Forronagh. They did so. They put out a small boat immediately from the ship, put the sailor into it, and left him ashore at Forronagh. He crept up the slope till he reached the edge. He sat down there, weak after his climb and very sick. There was a priest in Glen at that time, and he came to this district on a sick-call. From here, he had to go to Teelin then to hear confessions at a station. He and his clerk were walking up by Slieve League, and when they reached the top, at the mouth of the cave at Fogheray, they heard someone moaning.

'That's someone who is near death !' said the clerk.

He searched about and found a man sitting near the edge of the cliff. The priest approached him and asked him why he was there and where he had come from. He told the priest then how he had come from Spain.

'My mother asked me,' said he, 'to pray on my rosary beads every morning, if I could, that I would have a priest with me when I'd die.'

'You have one with you now, 'said the priest.

When the sailor had made his confession and the priest had anointed him, the priest and his clerk took him to a caretaker's house up on the mountain at the foot of Malinbeg. There they left him. He gave the belt and all the money to the priest and asked him to build a church with it. We have seen the two churches that the priest built, the one at Bunadreesrubaun and another small one at Farmacbride.

Legends concerning the origins of churches and other sacred edifices are numerous in Ireland. The 'station' mentioned refers to the holding of a religious service, including Mass, in private houses of a townland in turn ; the practice, probably a relic of the Penal Days, is still carried out in most areas of Ireland. The places mentioned in the legend are in South Donegal.

61 *The straight road*

There was a poor woman there one time, and she used to be travelling around looking for alms. She had a small little son. They were at Mass one day, and the priest said that anyone who followed the straight road would prosper. On their way home, the mother wanted to go around by the road they came, but the boy wouldn't go with her ; he said that they should go the straight way through the fields. As they were arguing, who came along to them but the priest, who was on his way home after saying Mass !

'What's the trouble, at all ?' he asked the mother.

'This blackguard doesn't want to come with me,' said she.

'Why wouldn't you go along with your mother, and do what she says ?' asked the priest.

'Of course, I'll go with her, but she must go the straight way,' said the boy.

'Isn't it all the same to you what way she takes ?' said the priest.

'Why did you say in your sermon, so, that anyone who followed the straight road would get on well ?'

The priest said nothing for a while. Then he asked the mother would she let the boy go with him, and he would rear him.

'You'd have your hands full trying to rear him, Father !' said she.

'Never mind ! Let him come with me, and I'll rear him.'

'I'll be glad to, Father,' said she, 'and may my blessing go along with him !'

The priest took the boy up on the horse in front of himself ; maybe he had a carriage, but I can't say. Then he ordered his housekeeper at home to give his own meals to the boy to serve him. So it was the boy who took the meals in to the priest always, when they were ready. There was a picture of Our Saviour – may He ever be praised ! – along the way that the boy passed with the meals, a kind of hall or somewhere, I suppose. Each time that the boy passed the picture, he used to leave some of the food for the Boy that was in it. Then on Christmas Eve, the Boy in the picture asked the little boy would he go to spend Christmas with Him. The little boy said that he would, if the priest allowed him to go.

'You can go to the priest so,' said the Boy, 'and if he lets you come, we'll have Christmas together tonight.'

The little boy went to the priest and asked him would he allow
him to go to spend Christmas with the little Boy outside.

'What little boy ?' asked the priest,

'The Boy that's outside there in the picture on the wall.'

'Did he speak to you ?'

'He asked me to spend Christmas with Him.'

'What influence have you with that boy ?' asked the priest.

'I haven't any, but I never brought food to you without giving
Him a little of it.'

'And used he to eat it ?'

'I don't know whether He did or not. I never made any delay,
only to give Him the food, but there was none of it left when I came
back from you.'

'Go out to him so, and tell him that I will allow you to go, if he
lets me go along with you,' said the priest.

The little boy went to the picture and told the Boy that the priest
would let him go, if He allowed the priest to go with him. The boy
returned to the priest and told him that he could go with him.

'When you are going to bed tonight, come to my room,' said the
priest.

He did, and the priest told him to lie near the wall on his bed.
On the morning of Christmas Day, the housekeeper thought that
they were getting up too late for Mass, so she went to call them. She
found the priest and the little boy dead in the bed. They had gone
to spend Christmas with the Boy.

For studies of this legend and for references to it, see Bolte-Polivka,
Anmerkungen III, 474 ; *PMLA*, XL, 93 ; *FFC*, XC, 90 ; Richmond,
Studies in Folklore, Szöverffy, 'A Medieval Story and its Irish Version',
pp. 55–65 ; Szöverffy, *Irisches Erzählgut*, 141-9.

62 *Conor mac Nessa*

Long ago people were few, and the priests used to travel about saying
Mass and spending a night here and there. Some of them arrived at
a house and they asked the boy to go out and cut some rushes with

a sickle to make a bed. The boy went out to a clump of rushes, and a voice spoke to him from out the clump :

'Don't put me out of my dwelling !'

The boy went away from the clump and told the priests in the house what had happened.

'Didn't you bring the rushes ?' they asked.

'No, Father,' said he to one of them. 'If I told you what I have heard, you wouldn't go there either !'

'Come along and show me where this was said.'

They went out to the clump. The priest put on his stole and read something, and a voice spoke from the clump.

'Who are you ?' asked the priest.

'I am Conor of Ulster,' said the voice.

'How long have you been here ?'

'Since the Saviour was crucified,' said the voice.

'And what put you here ?' asked the priest.

'It happened this way. I was in a battle, and a piece of something entered my skull. When I heard later on that the Saviour was crucified, frenzy came upon me. I went out into the woods with my sword, and the piece fell out of my skull, and I died. The Saviour then put my soul into my skull until the Day of Judgement.'

'I'll baptise you now, and you will go to Heaven,' said the priest.

'Must I die a second time ?' asked the voice.

'You must.'

'Oh, Father, I'd rather stay in my skull until the Day of Judgement !' said the voice.

When the priest heard these words, tears fell from his eyes down on the clump, and Conor of Ulster immediately rose up from it like an angel.

'I'm on my way to Heaven now, Father !' said he. 'Your tears have baptised me !'

Conor mac Nessa was said to have been king of the Ulstermen in the heroic age, when Cúchulainn was their great hero. As the legend indicates, he is supposed to have lived at the time of Christ. For a rather similar legend associated with the Crucifixion, see *A Manual,* Wells (155) ; also Szövérffy, *Irisches Erzählgut,* 86-96.

63 *Saints Colmkille and Enda*

Long ago, in the time of the saints, Colmkille was in Aran, and so was Saint Enda. Colmkille went and copied a book that Enda had, but when it was finished, Enda wanted 'to keep the copy as well as the book. There was anger and dispute about the copy ; Colmkille wanted to keep it, and that brought on war between the two sides. In the end, so great was the trouble that all the saints came together and punished Colmkille – he was banished from every place where he could hear Enda's bell ringing. So he had to leave Aran. He went down to the shore and stood on a stone there. The stone floated away, with Colmkille standing on it, until it reached Casla, on the Connemara side. There is a holy well, named after Colmkille, there ever since, and people from this county and from other counties come there on a pilgrimage on the ninth day of June.

Colmkille wasn't able to remain long in Casla, for he could hear Enda's bell every day when it rang in Aran. He set off for Derry in the province of Ulster and built a very large monastery there. He did a lot of work there for years and was very tired at the end of it. One fine day he was walking around the monastery, and what did he hear but the sound of Enda's bell ! So he said to himself that he would have to leave Derry. He would go to Scotland and make Christians of as many people there as had been killed in the fighting in Aran. That was good, and it wasn't bad ! He got ready for the journey to Scotland, and he told the monk who was with him that they could not travel by daylight or look behind because of all the hardship and trouble he had suffered. He would travel by night instead.

'You will wake me in the morning when you hear the cock crowing,' said Colmkille to the monk.

'I'll do that,' said the monk.

Night came. The monk didn't sleep a wink, but Colmkille slept well. When day was coming, the cock didn't crow until it was time for breakfast. The monk called Colmkille.

'Why didn't you call me when the cock crowed ?' asked Colmkille.

'The cock crowed only now,' said the monk.

'May Kilsallagh have no cock,' said Colmkille,

'And may the cock have no head,

And may no cock ever crow in Derry
Until that time of day !'
It is said that since that time, no cock has crowed in Derry until
ten o'clock in the morning.

Still, Colmkille decided that he would have to leave without delay.
He got a horse and saddled it. He mounted it, and the monk had
another horse. They rode on towards the seaport where a ship would
take them to Scotland. Colmkille told the monk to look behind him
to see what he could. He did so.

'I see a dark host all over Derry,' said the monk.

'Oh, Derry will have dark faith yet,' said Colmkille.

They rode on. They probably had a long way to go to the seaport
from which they could sail to Scotland. After another while,
Colmkille told the monk to look back again and to tell him what
he saw. The monk looked behind a second time and saw a great,
strong dog and a little spaniel fighting for a bone. The little spaniel
took the bone from the big dog and ran off with it. The monk told
Colmkille what he had seen.

'Oh, Ireland will belong to the Spaniards yet !' said Colmkille.

They reached the seaport and crossed over to Scotland. Colmkille
made Christians of twice as many people there as had been killed in
the war in Ireland on account of the book. He stayed in Scotland
until his death. He wished to die in Ireland, for his heart was there
and he wished that his body would be buried in Irish soil. Before he
died, he told the monk who was with him – it was he who had been
travelling about with him – to put his body, when he died, into a
stone coffin and to place it on the shore. That was done. The tide
covered the coffin every day. And it is said that the stone coffin, with
Colmkille's body inside, floated across the sea to Ireland and came
ashore in Derry.

A farmer who had a lot of cattle lived at that spot. We know that
when summer comes and the weather is warm, cattle run down to
the shore of the sea and go out into it to cool themselves. One of
the cows that belonged to this farmer started to eat the sea-weed that
grew on the coffin. Nobody knew what kind of stone it was. When
the cow had eaten all the sea-weed that was on the stone, she used
to start licking the stone, and each day she gave as much milk as did
the other four cows that were eating the grass. The herdsman noticed
how much milk she had and he kept his eye on her. Each day he

found her on the strand licking the same stone. He decided that the stone had some miraculous power, seeing that the cow had so much milk, without eating any grass every day, but only licking the stone. Other people joined him to watch the stone and the cow. They noticed that the stone had a top cover above the lower part, and the two were joined firmly together. They prised them apart, and found the body of Colmkille inside.

They took the body and decided that it should be buried along with Saint Patrick and Saint Bríd. When they brought it to that graveyard, where the two saints were buried, it is said that the two graves moved apart, leaving a space between them for Colmkille. The three of them are buried in the same graveyard.

The legendary 'battle of the books' between Saint Enda of Aran, County Galway, and Saint Colmkille, is well-known in the field of Irish hagiography. See Szövérffy *Irisches Erzählgut,* 97-136. The latter saint was later associated with the island of Iona, on the western coast of Scotland. A large body of legendry has surrounded his name. He is said to have been buried with Saints Patrick and Bríd in Downpatrick, County Down.

64 *Saint Colmkille's well*

Two men from this place went by boat to Galway one time. They left Galway very early next morning on the journey home. The day was calm, so they had to row. It was a long way, and they grew tired. One of them used to smoke a pipe, and he was badly in need of a smoke. He had his pipe and tobacco, but he had only one match.

'May God help me!' said he. ' 'Tis a long journey, and if I light the match now, I won't be able to take another smoke for the rest of the day. I'll wait another while.'

He tried his best to pass the day without a smoke, though he was 'dying' for one, for he wanted to save the match. They rowed on westwards. At last they had a slight breeze behind them, which barely stirred the sail, and the man put the pipe into his mouth, without 'reddening' it, to pretend that he was smoking.

'I'm so tormented,' he said at last, 'that I'll strike the match! I can't stand it any longer!'

He pulled out the pipe and the match and bent down to shade

them while he was 'reddening' the pipe. He smoked for a while, and then he remembered the mistake he had made. There is a holy well dedicated to Saint Colmkille near the shore to the west of Galway, and no boat-crew ever passed that well, either eastwards or westwards, without taking off their hats and going down on their knees and praying to Colmkille.

'May God help me!' said the man who was smoking. 'Here is the well, and I have only just "reddened" my pipe! I'll have to put it away till I get home sometime tonight, and my only match is gone!'

When they came to where the well was, he put aside his pipe on top of the locker, sorry that he had struck the match too soon. He went on his knees and prayed to Colmkille.

'I have no smoke at all now!' said he, when the prayer was over.

They travelled on. He didn't touch the pipe again, though he was 'dying' for a smoke. At last, after two or three hours, he took up his pipe from the locker and put it in his mouth, though it wouldn't do him much good. He started to 'pull' it, and at the first draw, he found that the pipe was as 'red' as it was when he had laid it aside! He took a good smoke, and thanked God and the Virgin Mary and Saint Colmkille a thousand times for the miracle which had kept the pipe 'red' for such a long time. He then laid the pipe aside.

The man to whom that happened told me the story himself. It is as true as what any man or woman has ever told. He told many other people about it also.

The dear blessing of God and of the Church on the souls of the dead! And may myself and this company be better a year from tonight!

Many holy wells in Ireland have the name of Saint Colmkille associated with them. The well mentioned in the present legend is on the south coast of Conamara, County Galway.

65 *Saint Patrick and Crom Dubh*

The last Sunday in July is called the Sunday of Crom Dubh (Black Crom) in this part of the country. Crom Dubh was a pagan, and that

Sunday is named after him because it was the day on which he
turned Christian in the time of Saint Patrick. Crom Dubh lived
somewhere in Connacht, maybe in Mayo, when Saint Patrick himself
was in Connacht. They lived near each other, and each of them knew
about the other. Saint Patrick used to be preaching sometimes, but
if he was, Crom Dubh wasn't ready yet to turn Christian. Still, they
were very good friends.

Crom Dubh sent his boy one time to Saint Patrick with a gift of
a quarter of beef that he had slaughtered. The boy took it to the
saint's house and told him that his master had sent him this present.

'Deo gratias!' ('Thanks be to God!') said the saint.

The boy went home to his master, Crom Dubh.

'Was Patrick very thankful to me for sending him the quarter of
beef?' asked Crom Dubh.

'I can't tell you that,' said the boy. 'I don't know was he thankful
to you, for I couldn't understand the words he said at all. I never
before heard anyone saying what he said. I don't know what it was.'

'I have another quarter here,' said Crom Dubh. 'Take it to him
and tell him it is a present from me. We'll see will he thank me for
the second quarter.'

The servant took along the second quarter to Saint Patrick and
told him that it was another present from his master.

'Deo gratias!' said Saint Patrick.

That was all that he said. The boy went back, and Crom Dubh
asked him:

'Did Patrick thank you for the second quarter that I sent him?'

'The same thanks as the first time,' said the boy. 'I don't know
from Adam what he said!'

'I have another quarter here, as well as the other two', said Crom
Dubh. 'I'll send it to him to see will he thank me for it. Take it to
him now!'

The boy took the third quarter and left it at Saint Patrick's house.

'Here's another quarter for you from my master,' said he.

'Deo gratias!' said Saint Patrick.

The boy returned to his master.

'Well, what kind of thanks did he give you for bringing the third
quarter?' asked Crom Dubh.

'He says the same words every time,' said the boy. 'I don't know,
for the life of me, what he said. 'Twas the same every time.'

'Off with you now,' said Crom Dubh, 'and order him to come here. Say that I'm inviting him, and not to delay!'

What Crom Dubh wanted him for was to kill him because he hadn't thanked him or gone on his knees to show gratitude for the third quarter of beef.

'I'll be with you,' said Saint Patrick to the boy. 'We mustn't delay. I'll be there as soon as you will.'

Saint Patrick went to Crom Dubh, and he was only inside the door when Crom Dubh asked him:

'What kind of thanks did you give me for the three quarters of beef that I sent you?'

'Oh, I thanked you heartily,' said Saint Patrick.

'You didn't thank me at all', said Crom Dubh.

'Indeed, I thanked you very much!' said Patrick. 'Have you weighing scales?'

'I have,' said Crom Dubh.

'Have you three quarters of beef as heavy as the three that you sent to me as presents?'

'I have,' said Crom Dubh.

'Put them on the scales,' said Patrick.

Patrick wrote the words *'Deo gratias!'* three times on a piece of paper. Crom Dubh put the three quarters of beef on one side of the scales, and Patrick laid the piece of paper on which he had written *'Deo gratias!'* three times on the other scale. The piece of paper weighed down that side of the scales, for it was much heavier than the three quarters of beef that Crom Dubh put in!

'Oh, Patrick!' said Crom Dubh. 'It is I who was wrong! Baptise me, for God's sake, and all of my household! They must become Christians today!'

And that is why the last Sunday in July is called the Sunday of Crom Dubh. 'Tis on that day that the huge crowd goes to Croagh Patrick in County Mayo. There is also a large 'pattern' at a place called Mám Éan, in the Twelve Bins of Connemara. Ever since, the Sunday of Crom Dubh commemorates the Sunday when the pagan, Crom Dubh, became a Christian at the time of Saint Patrick.

For references to Crom Dubh (Black Crom), see MacNeill, *The Festival of Lúghnasa,* where this legend and many others are mentioned. Saint Patrick flourished in Ireland in the fifth century, and to him the christianisation of the country is mainly credited. The legend

of *'Deo gratias'* ('Grazacham') was very popular in Irish oral tradition.
A 'pattern' (name derived from patron saint) was the name for a local
pilgrimage to a holy well associated with a saint.

All the places mentioned in the legend are in the Province of
Connacht, in the west of Ireland.

66 Saint Patrick and the tavern-woman

When Saint Patrick was in Iveragh – he never came here to
Corkaguiny – he was travelling along. One day he went into a tavern
and called for a pint. The woman went to the barrel, drew the pint
and handed it to him.

'Fill it!' said Saint Patrick.

She put another drop into it, but it wasn't filled yet.

'Fill it!' said Saint Patrick again.

She put another drop into it. And she had to do so three times
before it was full.

'Look over to your right,' said Saint Patrick to her.

She did and she saw a huge, fat dog on top of the barrel. At the
end of a year and a day, Saint Patrick passed that way again, and he
went into the same tavern and called for a pint. The woman filled
the pint up to the brim.

'Did you fill each pint like that during the past year?' Saint Patrick
asked her.

'I did,' said she.

'Look over to your right,' said Saint Patrick.

She did and she saw a small dog, whose bones were sticking out
through his skin, walking to and fro on top of the barrel.

This may have been used by preachers as an *exemplum,* its purpose
being to warn against dishonesty. The dog on the barrel, as is evident
from other versions, was the Devil, who was thriving on the
ill-gotten gains of the dishonest tavern-woman.

Iveragh and Corkaguiny are baronies in West Kerry.

67 *Saint Patrick curses Ireland*

When Saint Patrick was going to bed one time, he said to his servant boy:

'Take care now! I'm going to lie down and I may talk in my sleep. I greatly fear that what I say won't be very polite, so listen to everything I say!'

When Saint Patrick had slept for a while, he began to snore, and it wasn't long till he started to rave.

'Bad luck to Ireland!' he shouted in his sleep.

The boy was listening to him.

'If so, let it be on the tips of the rushes!' said he.

Saint Patrick slept on for another while, and began to rave again.

'Bad luck to Ireland!' said he.

The boy answered him.

'If so, let it be on the highest part of the white cows!' said he.

Saint Patrick slept for another while and spoke again in his sleep.

'I'll say again what I said twice already: "Bad luck to Ireland!" ' said he.

The boy answered him.

'If so, let it be on the bottom of the furze!' said he.

Saint Patrick awoke after a while.

'Did I say anything while I was asleep, boy?' he asked.

'You did,' said the boy,

'And what did I say?'

'You said: "Bad luck to Ireland!" three times!'

'And what did you say?'

'The first time you said it, I said: "If so, let it be on the tips of the rushes!" The second time you said it, I said: "If so, let it be on the highest part of the white cows!" And the third time you said it, I said: "If so, let it be on the bottom of the furze!" '

'You are the best boy that was ever in Ireland,' said Saint Patrick.

That's why every priest should have a boy serving him at Mass.

This is an aetological legend to explain *(a)* why the tips of the green rushes are withered: *(b)* why the tips of the horns of white cows are black; and *(c)* why the lower part of a furze bush is withered. The reason for the three characteristics given at the end of this legend is weak, as compared with the reasons more usually given, as above.

68(a) *Saint Martin's Eve*

Saint Martin's Eve comes nine nights after Hallowe'en. It is a custom to shed blood that night, or else a few nights or days before the Feast. 'Martin will accept the sacrifice before his Feast, but not after it', they say. No family should expect to be lucky during the following year if they do not shed blood that night. People kill geese, ducks, hens or something like that in order to shed the blood. It must be sprinkled in the four corners of the house. Fishermen who are at sea that night are very lucky; they make heavy catches. There is great virtue in shedding the blood as it brings much luck to the people of the house.

There was an old woman there long ago, and she owned nothing in the world. She was poor, badly dressed, cold and empty-handed. Saint Martin's Eve came around, and the poor woman was troubled as she had nothing to kill.

'May God and Christ and the Virgin Mary help me!' said she to herself. 'What will I do at all?'

A neighbouring woman called in to see her, and she advised her not to worry. It would make no difference, and Martin wouldn't blame her when she couldn't help it.

'For the love of Jesus Christ,' said the old woman, 'are you telling me I should break a law that all of my forefathers obeyed? I'll be far from breaking it!'

The next moment she took up a knife. And what did she do but cut off her small toe and go into the four corners of the house with the blood, without saying a word! Then she went joyfully to bed.

'Life lasts only for a while,' said she. 'The seed will last, but not the hand that sowed it.'

It is said that God does not fail His own children. And that is true, as this old woman can prove. She prospered. Money came to her in a big lump, as some relative of hers, who had never eaten his fill, died and had to leave her the thousand pounds that he had stored up. It was God Who sent it to her.

It is said that the first person who shed blood for Saint Martin was Saint Patrick, and it has been the custom ever since.

The Feast of Saint Martin is celebrated by the Church on 11 November.

For the way in which the Irish people traditionally observed it on the eve of the Feast Day, see Richmond, *Studies in Folklore*, 252-61. Ó Súilleabháin. 'The Feast of St. Martin in Ireland'.

68(b) *Saint Martin's Eve*

Long ago there was a man and his wife and they had one child. The man was very fond of cards and he was playing them somewhere always. He used to win money and other things too.

He wasn't at home on Saint Martin's Eve, and his wife was looking after the child. It was a rule in Ireland at that time, and so it is today, that blood should be shed for Martin. The old people say that Martin will accept it before his Feast-day, but not after it. This woman was sad as she had nothing to kill that night, and she knew that Martin wouldn't accept it later on. She had the child in the cradle. A notion struck her that she would draw a drop of blood from the child's finger. She cut the finger with a knife, and blood came. Finally she couldn't stop the blood, and the child died.

After a while, a travelling man came in to her and asked her for lodgings for the night. She said that she hadn't much room, but she'd try to keep him. She did. She was working about the house and was very sad at heart. Later on in the night, her husband returned with a fine piece of meat which he had won in a card-game. He had great welcome for the stranger and asked his wife to get supper ready. She did. When they were about to sit down to eat, the husband asked the woman where was the child. She said he was asleep.

'No matter,' said he. 'I won't eat anything until you bring him to me.'

The poor woman knew that she was in trouble.

'Oh,' said the stranger, 'take up the child for his supper.'

She went over to where the child was and found him fast asleep and perspiring! She threw herself on her two knees and thanked God and the night that it was. She told her husband about the child. They ate the supper more happily than she had expected. When they had eaten, the stranger told them that he was Saint Martin and that it was he who had raised the child from the dead. He asked the man of the house what trade he had, and was told that it was card-playing.

'Play them fairly,' said Saint Martin, 'and nobody will be better than you in this world or in the next from this night forward.'

And then the saint vanished from their sight again. The husband spent the rest of his life playing cards, and no one could beat him. When the day came that he was to leave this world, he told them to put the pack of cards into the coffin with his body, and they did so. He went straight up to Heaven, but when he arrived at the gate, Saint Peter wouldn't let him in unless he left the cards outside.

'Where am I to go then?' asked the man.

'Go down to the place below,' said Saint Peter.

Down he went, and the man below had great welcome for him, of course. He was roasting two souls on the fire. He asked the card-player what he wanted. He told the Devil that he had been to Heaven, but that he wouldn't be let in on account of the cards. He said that he would wager his own soul to free the two souls that were on the fire. The Devil said that he was satisfied to play against him. They began to play, and he beat the Devil and won the two souls. Who were they but the souls of his father and mother! They went up to Heaven immediately. They played on, and he won a large number of souls. Finally the Devil banished him from Hell. He went up to Heaven's gate again, but Saint Peter wouldn't let him in unless he left the cards outside. He returned to this world and came to a man who was stealing turf at the side of a road. The poor man fainted – he thought that he had been caught in the act.

'Get up!' said the ghost of the card player. 'You're in no danger from me!'

He then told the man that he had been to Heaven and to Hell, but couldn't stay in either place because of the cards.

'Here they are for you!' said the ghost. 'Play them fairly, and nobody will be able to beat you as long as you live.'

The ghost went up to Heaven again and he had no delay in getting in this time. He's still in Heaven. Didn't he fare well with the Devil when he was in Hell!

See note to previous legend.

VII
Individual Persons

It is only natural that in all ages, and in every district, particular individuals, for one reason or another, became almost folk figures and gathered around them legends which might not have been told about them at all in the first instance. Dean Swift, Oliver Cromwell, Daniel O'Connell and hundreds of poets as well as thousands of others have an important place in Irish legendry. From such a long list, only a few can be chosen for mention here.

69 *Caoilte the swift*

There was a king in Ireland long ago. Each morning sand from the four quarters had to be brought to him: the west strand, the east strand, the upper strand and the lower strand. And the king could tell by looking at the sands whether any enemy was coming to attack his country. He had a servant boy who brought the sand to him every morning. The boy died, and when he was buried three applied for the job immediately. One of them said that he could do the work, if he got the job.

'How long would it take you to bring me the sand each morning?' asked the king.

'Only as long as it would take a leaf to fall from a tree,' said he.

'Oh, you wouldn't be quick enough! I won't take you,' said the king. 'How long would it take you?' he asked the second man.

'Only as long as it would take a cat to go from one house to another.'

'You wouldn't be quick enough either,' said the king.

The third man was Caoilte.

'How long would the job take you?' asked the king.

'Only as long as it would take a woman to change her mind,' said Caoilte.

'Have you done the job yet, Caoilte?' asked the king.

'I have, and here I am!' said Caoilte.

This legend is rooted in lore of the Fianna, the warriors led by Finn mac Cool, of whom Caoilte was reputed as being the swiftest and, like Oisín, to have lived on to meet Saint Patrick in Christian times. Tests in speed were a common theme in folktales and legends.

70 *Cahal of the red hand*

It was Cahal of the Red Hand that built this monastery at Ballin-tubber. He was the son of the great Turlough O'Connor, king of

Connacht; his mother was not the queen but a woman of the Morans from Kilmeena in Umhall Í Mháille.

When the queen heard that this child was to be born, she started to worry about her own children, because there was a prophecy that King Turlough would have a son in this way who would become king of Connacht later on. The queen sent for the hen-hag to make a charm that would prevent this child from being born or cause the death of his mother and himself. The hag came and made the charm and said that the child would not be born while it remained in the queen's possession.

Time went by until the poor mother was to give birth to her child. She was unable to do so, however, because of the evil magic of the queen, and everybody feared that there was no remedy for her. The child's hand appeared, but the rest of its body didn't.

In those days there was a pedlar travelling throughout Connacht. He heard that the poor Moran woman was near death and that she would die unless the black spell of the queen upon her was broken. He set off across the country and never stopped till he made off the king's castle in Roscommon. He got into conversation with the young women who were working in the kitchen, and gave them presents to show to their mistress. When the queen heard that such a visitor was in the castle, she sent for him to come to her room. She asked him where he came from.

'From west in Mayo,' he replied.

'Have you any news from that place?' she asked.

'I have, a little, but I'd be slow to mention such a thing to you,' said he.

'Tell me your news,' said the queen, 'and I promise that you won't be blamed in any way for it.'

'What was on everybody's lips when I left,' said the pedlar, 'was that a young son had been born to the king on a certain day.'

That took a start out of the queen.

'Are you sure that's true?' she asked, and her eyes were almost jumping out of their sockets.

'As sure as that I'm standing here,' said the roguish pedlar.

'If that's the way things are,' said she, white with anger, 'there's no use my keeping this any longer!'

She started to her feet and threw a small slender rope of silk that she had in a box into the fire.

'May the Devil take that charm and the woman who made it!' said she.

The charm lost its power as soon as the rope took fire. The poor mother who was dying got relief, and the child was born. A fine male child he was, but, God bless the mark! one of his hands was as red as blood, and so it remained ever afterwards. When he grew up he used always wear a glove, but everybody knew about the red hand. That's why he was nicknamed Cahal of the Red Hand, and the name had clung to him ever since.

That was that. The mother and her son had survived the danger. The queen didn't remain idle, but was looking for any chance to put the child to death. The mother had to flee from her home and the poor creature went through a lot of suffering, as she slipped from place to place with her little son in fear that the queen might catch him. When Cahal grew up, he used to spend his time working here and there, and nobody knew who he was. It is said that he spent two years here in Ballintubber, working for a man named Sheridan. This man was good and kind to Cahal, and when he was leaving the district, Cahal told his master that until the day of his death he would not forget his kindness.

Time passed, and it fell to Cahal to become king of Connacht. They say that he was working for a farmer east in Leinster when he was called to the throne. He was reaping rye when the messengers arrived in quest of him. The farmer, of course, didn't know him from Adam! Cahal threw his sickle up into the air.

'Farewell now to the sickle,' said he, 'and welcome the sword!'

He pulled off the glove, showed his red hand to the messengers, and went off with them.

That was that. It happened that Cahal, when he was king, passed through Ballintubber one time, and he called in to Sheridan to see how his old friend was. It is no lie to say that Sheridan was surprised at the great change that had come over his workman since he had left him. Cahal spoke kindly to him and said he would give him anything he asked for.

'An old man like me doesn't need much,' said Sheridan. 'But the people of this place are in need of a church; the old one is on the point of falling down on top of us!'

'I'll give orders that a church be built in Ballintubber without delay,' said Cahal.

A couple of years went by, and the church wasn't built. All the people were wondering why the king hadn't kept his promise. It chanced that the king was passing that way again and he called to see his old friend and asked him did he need anything.

'Don't be slow in asking,' said the king. 'You'll get what you want, and welcome!'

'The person who doesn't ask isn't in danger of being refused,' said the old man, rather resentfully.

'What's that you're saying? What's wrong?' asked the king.

'We were promised a church, but it hasn't been built yet,' said Sheridan.

'You're wrong in that, my good man!' said the king. 'I gave orders to have a church built in Ballintubber, and was told that it had been built.'

'I'm not wrong at all,' said Sheridan. 'Ballintubber is still without a church.'

The king was astonished. He enquired from his servants and found out that it was in Ballintubber in Roscommon that the church had been built! So he gave orders a second time that a church be built in Ballintubber in Mayo.

'And fine though the church that was built in the other place is, the church here must be seven times finer!' the king told his workmen.

The masons set to work, and 'tis no lie to say that they built a fine church! It is still standing after hundreds of years, and has been used as a church by the people of Ballintubber from the day it was built until now. That's a story that can't be told about any other church in Ireland!

The chief character in this legend 'Cahal More of the Wine-red Hand', is mentioned by the poet, James Clarence Mangan, in 'A Vision of Connacht in the Thirteenth Century'. Cahal Crovdearg (of the Red Hand), King of Connacht, is said to have founded an abbey in Ballintubber, County Mayo, in 1216, for Canons Regular of Saint Augustine. Though wrecked by the Cromwellians, Mass continued to be celebrated there ('in the abbey that refused to die') and the abbey was fully restored in 1966, on its 750th anniversary.

All of the places mentioned are in the Province of Connacht.

71(a) *Grace O'Malley*

Grace O'Malley had a son, and he was a prisoner of the Flaherties in their castle at Renvyle. One day, she sailed into Renvyle Harbour in a big ship. She gave birth to a child there, and the same day, after the child was born, she got out of bed and hoisted her flags, telling the Flaherties that she would knock the castle to the ground, if they didn't let her son go free. The son was released and he went out to the ship. But Grace was still so angry with the Flaherties that she fired a cannon-ball at the castle and knocked down the wing of it.

> Grace O'Malley (Gráinne Ní Mháille, Granuaile), a famous woman of County Mayo, is said to have been born about 1530. She first married Donal O'Flaherty and later Richard Burke. Bingham referred to her as 'the nurse of all the rebellions in the province (of Connacht) for forty years'. She is said to have visited Queen Elizabeth I in London. She died about 1600. Many legends and much other lore are associated with her name, which, as Granuaile, became a synonym for Ireland.
>
> Renvyle is in County Mayo.

71(b) *Grace O'Malley*

The Red-haired Smith was the finest man was ever seen. He was the brother of Grace O'Malley. She was very proud of him, and she thought that even her own husband, a man named Burke, wasn't as fine a man as her brother. Her husband told her to have some sense, that himself was twice as fine, but she said that none of his race was better than her brother.

'I'll prove to you that I'm a better man, the next time he calls here,' said the husband.

When the Red-haired Smith came later on, they ate dinner, and then the husband told him that his wife had insulted him by saying that her brother was a better man.

'I'm sure that I'm better than you,' said the Red-haired Smith.

Each of them drew his rapier and they went out in front of the castle. Within a half-hour, the husband had cut off the head of the Red-haired Smith. He took hold of the head by his left hand and, holding his rapier in his right, he marched in to his wife, the sister of the dead man.

'Here's the head of the Red-haired Smith for you now ! said he. 'Shed all the tears you wish over it !'

She had two fine sons in their teens at that time. They were outside in the garden amusing themselves. She went out and called them into the parlour where she was. She took hold of her rapier and cut off their two heads. She took hold of the two heads by the hair and made her way to her husband.

' 'Tis your turn to cry now !' said she. 'While you weep for your two sons, I'll weep for my brother, the Red-haired Smith.'

See note to the previous legend.

72 *The McDonnell headstone*

I heard the story told by a very old man here they called Hughie McGowan, and he had it from old people himself, he said, and he said it was a true story. The McDonnell headstone in the graveyard has a Red Hand, and he said this was how it all came about. McDonnell and McQuillan were both after the same girl. She was an O'Cahan, and in them times, when that happened, two after the one woman, the remedy, it seems, was to fight with swords. She wouldn't have that. Instead, she said they would have to race for her. So the two of them got into small boats and the race started. I think Hughie McGowan said that McDonnell was winning, but to make doubly sure, he ups with the sword and chopped off his hand and threw it on the rocks – that was the Pans Rock at Ballycastle, Carrig Ussna. And that's why on the McDonnell stone you get the Red Hand, the Fish and the Boat.

73 *The woman who chose her brother*

There was a woman there long ago at the time when Doncha Browne was hanging people, and her husband, her son and her brother were to be hanged. Blake of Athenry had the power of saving three persons from the gallows each year. He was in the court that day.

'Now,' said he to the woman, 'you can save one of them from hanging today. Which of them do you choose ?'

'Well,' said she, 'I can get a husband in Tuam, I can get a son from my womb, but I can never again get a brother.'

She chose her brother, and all three were freed.

For references to the theme of this legend in ancient Greek and Oriental sources, see *Éigse* I (1939), Michael Tierney, who says that only in Ireland is the motif found elsewhere. A number of versions of the legend, collected in Ireland, are published in *Éigse* II (1940), 24-30.

74 *Bonnie Prince Charlie*

When Prince Charles was on the run long ago he came to Mountcharles. He went into a forge there to get his horse shod and he asked the smith to put on the shoes backwards. The smith did this, and Charles mounted the horse and rode off. His pursuers were on his heels, but when they saw the way the shoe-tracks were pointing, they changed their course and went in the opposite direction.

Charles went on to Malinbeg and from there to Malinmore. He hid for a while there in a place called Folach Éireann (the Secret Place of Ireland). He then went on to Meenacrusha and hid there for a couple of nights.

At that time the English language was not known at all in that glen, and when he had taken his supper in the house where he was to spend the night, the people didn't know how they would tell him to go to bed. The woman of the house thought for a while. She spread out a floor-bed near the wall and then said to him : 'Bed, sir. I have prepared sleep for you.' When he was asleep, she said to one of the family : 'He's asleep now, and there isn't enough English in Meenacrusha to wake him, except I rouse him myself !'

When he awoke in the morning, she got his breakfast ready for him, and when he had eaten it, she understood by what words of English he spoke that he wanted tobacco. She filled a pipe for him. While she was doing so, he stretched himself like a tired or sleepy person would and said : 'Oh dear ! Oh dear !' 'Oh,' said she, 'whether 'tis dear or cheap, I'll fill this pipe for you '

He went from Meenacrusha to Glenlacha and boarded a ship at a place called Poll an Uisce (The Water-hole), and he wasn't seen again.

There is a strong folk tradition that Prince Charles Edward (1720–88), 'The Young Pretender', took refuge in Glencolmkille, County Donegal, from his pursuers. Whether he did or not, the story is told to show the difficulty people may have in making themselves understood by someone who does not speak their language. The English word 'dear' as a term of affection, when uttered by the prince, was understood by the woman as the Irish word *'daor'*, which means expensive.

The places mentioned are in the district of Glencolmkille in South Donegal.

75 *Damer*

When the people of Cashel heard that Cromwell was coming, they knew that he would rob the chapels and monasteries and the convents, so they collected all the sacred vessels and all the treasures belonging to the Church and put them into a barrel of tallow, thinking that that was the safest possible place to hide them. The barrel was mounted on a cart and taken down to a tallow-merchant's shop and rolled in, and nobody was any the wiser except the few who were in the know. The barrel was put by itself outside the counter and marked : Sold. To Be Called For. But whether it was sold or not, it didn't matter when Cromwell's men wanted it.

Damer was a chandler in Cromwell's army. It was his business to buy the tallow and make the candles. He went to Thurles one day and went into the tallow-merchant's store. He was feeling the barrels and picking out the heaviest ones. He came on one very heavy cask standing by itself, and he said to himself he'd have that one anyway. So when there was nobody looking, he rolled it over and put it in the middle of the barrels he had picked out. He paid his bill and loaded the tallow on his mules. He was barely gone when the owner of the store missed the barrel. But what could he do ? It was gone with Cromwell's soldiers ; it was a case of 'good day to you!' That's how Damer started collecting his gold.

When he got back to the camp, he opened the barrel in his tent. He smelted the chalices and the other vessels as best he could and hid the gold in big lumps of wax and tallow. He carried it all about with him till he got a chance of hiding it in a safe place. He hid it in a hollow tree in Lattin or Shronell, and that's why he selected land there when the divide was made. When men were cutting down that tree years and years after, some lumps of gold or coins fell out of it, and there were some smaller pieces found in jackdaws' nests around the place. A jackdaw will carry off anything bright: a scissors, a thimble, a pair of specs or even a wedding ring.

When the war was over, Damer got a big estate in Lattin and Shronell. He built a great house there, Damerville, the largest house in the British Isles at one time, with the exception of Windsor Palace. Scotchmen he had building the mansion. He brought them over from Scotland and when the work was over he kept them to work on the estate.

But of the great house there is no trace except the gable of a stable. What happened to the stones of the building, is it? They were carted all over the country to build chapels and churches, walls and houses.

Damer's grave is in one of the fields, but I never saw it. He was the richest man in Ireland. There is nobody that hasn't heard 'as rich as Damer'.

Joseph Damer (1630-1720) was, in Irish legendry, one of the wealthiest men in the country. 'As rich as Damer' was a common expression among the people. He was born in England, served in Cromwell's army, and in 1662 acquired an estate at Shronell in County Tipperary. He became a banker and usurer. For another legend about him, see O'Sullivan, *Folktales of Ireland*, No. 49, 240-2.

76(a) *Daniel O'Connell*

A man was returning home from Tralee one time after being working there as a migrant labourer. He was married and had a large family, poor man. He left Tralee at dawn in the morning, after spending three months there setting potatoes. He put his spade over his shoulder when he got his small wages and came to a house on the east side of Glenbeigh. He had two dozen potatoes in his pocket and he asked the woman of the house for a 'warmer' to boil the potatoes in.

'I don't have to give it to you at all,' said she. 'I have potatoes boiled already for the supper for the boys who are out working.'

She gave him potatoes and fish, and he left the cold potatoes with her. A travelling woman came in while he was there.

'As light as my spade is, I'm getting tired from it,' said he to the woman of the house, 'and, by heavens, I'll leave it behind me here, even though I may never see it again.'

'The spade will be quite safe, if you wish to leave it here,' said the woman of the house, 'until you pass this way again looking for work.'

'Are you a migrant labourer?' asked the travelling woman. 'That's what I am,' said he.

'The spade is your only weapon of defence, poor man,' said she. 'There's many a chance of your being attacked between here and Ballinskelligs.'

What she said set him thinking about the small amount of wages he had in his pocket. He threw his spade across his shoulder, bade them goodbye, and set out on his journey. As he was passing west by Drong Hill at twilight in the evening, he saw, coming towards him, a man who had something like an iron pistol in his hand. The stranger boldly ordered him to hand over his money. All that the labourer did was to draw a blow with the spade on him. The stranger fell down dead. The labourer looked behind him and thought that he caught sight of a 'peeler' (policeman), so he ran as fast as he could. His hat fell off, and he didn't try to get it back, in order to escape the peeler. He reached his home at Reenroe that night, on a Monday. He was arrested on the following Wednesday and brought before a police court. A peeler gave evidence that this man was guilty. The case was put back until the Sessions in May. He was certain that he would be hanged. He went to the Counsellor, Daniel O'Connell, and told him that he had killed a man who had tried to rob him of his wages.

'I was angry when he tried to rob me,' said he, 'but, when I struck him, I didn't think I'd kill him. My hat flew off, and the peeler who followed me has it now. I'm afraid that any court I go to will find me guilty.'

'Is your name on the hat?' asked O'Connell.

'Neither my name nor my surname is on it, or even the name of the makers', said the labourer.

'We may have a chance of getting our own back on that peeler so,' said O'Connell.

On the day of the trial, the case was called. The peeler had the hat on the bench, and O'Connell asked him to hand it to him. The peeler said that this was the man who had killed the other; he had seen him doing it. The attorney demanded a verdict of guilty.

'I think that you have right on your side,' said O'Connell to the peeler.

He picked up the hat and looked inside it.

'I see this man's name and surname inside. Did you see them?' he asked the peeler.

'Indeed I did.'

'Read them for me now,' said O'Connell.

The peeler was caught, and the labourer was freed.

Daniel O'Connell (1775-1847) was born at Carhan, near Caherciveen, in County Kerry. He was famous not only as a national leader, who won Catholic Emancipation of the Irish people, but also as a lawyer. So famous was he that he bacame a character even in some folktales, and a very large number of legends surrounded his name.

76(b) *Daniel O'Connell*

There was a poor man in it one time. He had five or six cattle and he was going to the fair with them. There was a shopkeeper living on the side of the road and he used to be doing a bit of dealing in cattle. When he saw the poor man coming, he stepped out in front of him on the road and began to buy the cattle. The six cattle weren't what you might call 'even' cattle to. They weren't all matches, and the poor man was expecting to sell them in ones and twos; he never expected to sell them all in one bunch.

'Well,' says the shopkeeper, 'how much for the good and the bad of them?'

The poor man thought that 'twas the best one and the worst one he meant, so he asked what he thought was a reasonable price. The shopkeeper gave him all he asked. He took the raddle out of his pocket and marked the whole bunch of cattle together.

'Stop!' says the poor man. 'I only sold two to you, the best and the worst.'

'You are a damn liar!' says the shopkeeper, 'I asked you for the good and the bad of them, and that's the whole bunch of cattle together. You can go to law any day you like, and I'll beat you in the law.'

'Twas the end of the story that the poor man had to go home with the price of only two of his cattle in his pocket. The rogue of a shopkeeper had him cheated out of the rest. He told the wife his story.

'If I was you,' says she, 'I wouldn't let much grass grow under my feet until I'd go as far as Daniel O'Connell and tell him my story.'

So next day he struck out for the hotel where Daniel O'Connell was staying, and in he goes and tells Daniel O'Connell his story.

'Your best won't beat him in the law,' says Daniel O'Connell, 'and what are you coming to me for when you have no case?'

'Ah, but, sir, you know in your heart that the rogue has me wronged. Could you do anything at all for me that I might knock my own out of him?'

Daniel took pity on the poor wretch, and he began to think and to re-think. Then he looked at the poor man.

'Well,' says he, 'how would you like if I cut off the tops of your two ears?'

'I wouldn't mind it a bit, if you could gain anything for me by doing it,' says the poor man.

'Tell me,' says Daniel, 'have you any friends over in England, or is there anyone belonging to you over in England?'

'Oh, there is ! There's a good deal of friends belonging to me working over in England.'

'Well,' says Daniel, 'I'm going to cut the tops off your ears now and I'll put them into a box and I'll post them to one of your friends beyond in England, if you tell me the address.'

So he told Daniel the address, and Daniel took his razor and he cut the tops off his two ears, and bandaged his ears again. Then he parcelled up the tops of the ears in a box and posted them off to the friend in England, and told him to take good care of the parcel for one month at least. The poor man was getting puzzled, and sure 'twas no blame to him!

'What's it all about, sir?' says he.

'I'll tell you that now,' says Daniel. 'Does that shopkeeper sell tobacco ?'

' 'Musha troth, 'tis nearly all tobacco that man is selling.'

'So he wouldn't make any wonder of selling you a few yards of it, would he ?' says Daniel.

'Not in the least, sir !' says the poor man.

'Well,' says Daniel, 'myself and yourself will go as far as that shop tomorrow, and I'll go in in disguise and I'll ask for something. Then you'll ask for as much tobacco as would go from the tops of your toes to the tops of your ears. He'll give a look at your height and he'll make a guess at all you'll want. And he'll charge you so much, and you'll pay him down every shilling of the money. Take the tobacco then, all he gives you. Be sure that you'll have your hat pulled down over the tops of your ears. Hold the tobacco then in your hand and say : "That's only a bit of the tobacco! Where is the rest of it ?" '

'He'll say that he gave you all you asked for, and you'll tell him that he didn't. He'll start to curse and swear that he did. And then you'll take off your hat and tell him that the tops of your ears are beyond in England. He'll say that you are only telling lies. I'll be there as your witness, ready to swear that I posted them over to such a one in England. He'll know that he's bet then and he'll try to make a settlement with you, but you'll make no settlement until you get all you ask'.

So next day the two walked in to the shopkeeper. Daniel bought a box of snuff, and then the poor man asked for as much tobacco as would go from the tops of his toes to the tops of his ears. The shopkeeper measured him with his eye and gave him about two yards of tobacco and charged him so much. The poor man paid down the money and took the tobacco and looked at it.

'Where is the rest of it, sir ?' says he.

'But you have it all there,' says the shopkeeper.

'I haven't it all there,' says the poor man, taking off his hat. 'I asked you for as much tobacco as would go from the tops of my toes to the tops of my ears, but you never asked where the tops of my ears were. The tops of my two ears are beyond in England.'

'That's a damn lie for you !' says the shopkeeper.

'There's a man in the corner that's ready to swear that he posted them over to England for me,' says the poor man.

Daniel swore on the spot that he did and that, if he went over to such a man in such a place in England, he'd get the tops of the two ears beyond. The shopkeeper turned black and blue in the face.

'Ye are two mean scoundrels !' says he to them.

'We aren't half as mean, and as big rogues as yourself were when you bought my six cattle for the price of two !' says the farmer. 'And what day are you going to stand the law with me ?'

'I'll stand no law at all with you, but I'll make a settlement here with you. I won't go any place else,' says the shopkeeper.

'This man here will draw up a settlement between us,' says the farmer.

Daniel O'Connell threw off the disguise and drew up the settlement, that the shopkeeper would have to pay out so many hundred pounds to the farmer. And I suppose that Daniel got a nice *brabach* (profit) out of it too – a thing he earned well !

See note to the previous legend.

77 *Aristotle and the bees*

As clever as Aristotle was, there was one thing that went beyond him all his life, and that was how did the bees make the honey. He tried every plan and couldn't find out. So at last he made a glass hive and put the bees into it. 'Now,' says he, 'whether they like it or not, I'll

find out how they make the honey !' But when he came to the hive
the next day to watch them making it, 'tis how they had plastered
it all over inside with wax, and he couldn't see a bit.

He was so vexed that he hit it a kick and broke it. All the bees
flew out and stung him and blinded him. He went away travelling
then, and he blind, and no one had any *meas* (regard) for him
because he was blind, and he had no *meas* on himself because he
couldn't find out how the bees made the honey. He lived the rest of
his life in a *botháinín* (little house) with three old men, and they
joking the clever man that tried to be clever enough for the bees.

In Irish legendry, Aristotle (384–322 BC), the great Greek
philosopher, was said to have been brother to the Barrscológ, another
character in Irish oral tradition, and that he was one of the wisest
men who ever lived. Only three things were said to have been beyond
his understanding : the secret workings of the bees, the ebbing and
flowing of the tide and the mind of a woman.

78 *King Brian Boru and the Danish heather ale*

It was when Brian Boru was king of Ireland that the Danish beer
was being made. There is a kind of a heather that is called Danish
heather ; it grows as a small clump, with short stems underneath.
The Danes used to be making this beer, and Brian was anxious to
find out how it was made. He captured some of those who were at
it one night and took them to his palace. He told them he wouldn't
let them go free until they told him the secret recipe. They were
hungry then for a time, but still it was no use being at them, so
Brian told them that they would never again see the light of day. He
then put them into a dark prison. Some of them were getting
dissatisfied, of course, and one old Dane among them was afraid that
the others would give away the secret. The next time that the butler
came to them with their food, the old man called him over and said
that he wanted to see Brian, the king. Word was sent to Brian and

he ordered the butler to bring the old Dane before him. This was done.

'Well,' said the old man to Brian, 'I will tell you the secret of the beer if you kill the others.'

'Why should I kill them ?' asked Brian.

'For fear that they would kill me for telling you the secret.'

'That will be done,' said Brian.

The rest of the Danes were killed. Brian then went to this old man that was left and asked him how the beer was made.

'If you're depending on me to tell you, you'll be without it, so you can kill me too,' said the old man.

He was killed, and ever after the secret knowledge was not found.

King Brian Boru (Brian of the Tributes) was killed in the year 1014 while leading his army against the 'Danes' at the Battle of Clontarf, near Dublin. For a version of 'The Heather Ale', O'Sullivan, see *Folktales of Ireland,* 234–5, and accompanying note. For some printed versions of the legend, see *Béaloideas* V (1935), 28–51, and *Festschrift till E. A. Kock,* 377, C. W. von Sydow 'Niebelungendiktningen och sägen om "An bheoir lochlannach" ; also *Arv* 21 (1965), 115-135, Bo Almqvist, 'The Viking Ale and the Rhine Gold'.

VIII
Robbers and Pirates

Highwaymen have inspired a large number of legends because of a kind of glamour which people associated with their lives. Some of these legends may be true, or have some basis of fact, and, of course, they lose nothing in the telling. Sometimes the same exploit is told about more than one highwayman, and thus becomes migratory. Whether the popularity of these men can be attributed to the people's hatred for unjust laws and tyrannical landlords, or whether some, at least, of the high-waymen did, in reality, rob the rich to help the poor is a matter for investigation by psychologists and historians.

79 *Redmond O'Hanlon*

Long ago the farmers used to take their butter to Cork to sell it. There were no carts there then, only firkins on the backs of horses. They used to have two firkins full of butter every year.

There was a farmer who had three sons. He asked the eldest son to tackle the horse and take the firkins to Cork. He refused, and so did the next son. The youngest son was a half-fool ; he had no great sense.

'I'll go, father,' said he.

' 'Tis no use for you to go, you little blackguard,' said the father. 'Redmond O'Hanlon, the great robber, would take the money off you on the way home.'

'Never mind,' said the son. 'Let me go !'

They gave in to him. They had an old horse that they had put out into a field to die. The youngest son brought in the horse and got ready for the road. Night was coming on as he was nearing Cork. There was a big bridge on the road, and Redmond O'Hanlon was standing there.

'Where are you making for, boy ?' he asked.

'To Cork to sell butter,' said the boy.

'You're a good boy,' said O'Hanlon. 'Will you come back this way tonight ?'

'I will, indeed !' said the boy.

He went into Cork and sold the butter. The butter-man told him that it was too late to set out for home ; he should wait until morning.

'I won't,' said the boy. 'The night is long and fine.'

'The big robber will take your money,' said the butter-man.

'There's no danger of that,' said the boy.

He got the money and knotted it into the lower part of his shirt. He set out. On the way, he collected a handful of shells on a river-bank, put them into a white bag, put a cord on it and set it in front of him on the horse. The robber was waiting for him at the bridge.

'You're here, boy !' said he.

'I am.'

O'Hanlon pulled a small revolver out of his pocket and told the boy to get down from the horse quickly.

'What's wrong with you ?' asked the boy. 'Why don't you take it easy ?'

The robber pulled him off the saddle.

'Hand over the money, boy !' said he.

The boy caught hold of the bag of shells and threw it over the wall of the bridge.

'I had the trouble of coming to Cork to get this money and I'll give you trouble too before you get it. Go and find it now !' said the boy.

O'Hanlon had a fine horse, and when he went down below the bridge to get the money, as he thought, the boy jumped on the robber's horse and galloped off. He left his old horse for O'Hanlon and took the young one. When the robber came up with the bag and opened it, he found only the shells. The boy went home to his father and mother and gave them the money.

'Where did you get that horse ?' asked the father. 'We'll be hanged for it !'

'Don't worry, father ! This horse is mine now,' said the boy.

Things stayed like that for a year until one day a poor man came to the farmer's house and asked for lodgings for the night. The farmer said that he wouldn't take in anybody like that ; there was a house at the top of the hill where he could stay.

'Send your little boy with me to show me the way,' said the poor man.

The boy went along with him. They sat down at the top of the hill, and the poor man asked the boy to pull off his old trousers. The boy did so.

'Isn't that a fine leg for an old man ?' said the beggarman.

' 'Tis,' said the boy.

'Do you recognise me ?'

'I don't,' said the boy.

'Indeed, you do !' said the beggarman. 'That was a good trick you played on me a year ago when you stole my fine horse and left me a bag of shells instead of money ! I'm going to shoot you now.'

'Don't !' said the boy, 'I'll be a good servant to you yet. We'll join together.'

At that time the bank where the farmers kept their money was a hole under the hearth-stone.

'Come with me now to my father's house, and I'll steal all his money,' said the boy.

'Good !' said O'Hanlon. 'You're a good boy.'

'You must stay outside and I'll go in,' said the boy. 'I'll call you in when they're asleep.'

That was good and it wasn't bad ! When the people of the house were asleep, the boy called in O'Hanlon. They lifted up the hearth-stone and the boy went down into the hole. There was a pile of money there. The boy filled a sackful and told O'Hanlon that it was too heavy for him to lift. He went up, and O'Hanlon took his place in the hole. All the boy did was to close the hole with the hearth-stone.

'I have caught you now, after all your robbing !' said the boy.

He called his father and told him that he had the big robber a prisoner under the hearth-stone. The father sent for the police and the boy got five pounds reward. O'Hanlon was hanged. The boy took his horse and let the bridle lie loose, so that the horse would guide him to O'Hanlon's house. The horse made his way over a high mountain and never stopped till he reached the house. It was full of gold and silver. The boy and his family took it all and lived happily ever after.

O'Hanlon was a 'Tory' (highwayman) of the Fews Mountains near Newry, who for ten years kept the counties of Armagh, Down and Tyrone in subjection. He was shot dead in April 1681, and is buried near Tanderagee, County Armagh. For an account of his exploits see *J.R.S.A.I.* IX (1867), 57-68 ; Carleton, *Redmond Count O'Hanlon,* 1-200 ; O'Hanlon, *The Highwayman in Irish History,* 32-49.

80 *William Crotty*

The old people used to say that Crotty the Robber had a stable for his stallion in a deep glen in the Comeragh mountains called Glenabisheeny. They said that a bootful of gold was hidden under the threshold of the stable. The army was hunting of Crotty one time. They tracked him to the lake, but he escaped down a hole and they couldn't find him. They spent three days waiting to see would the hunger drive him out, but it didn't. Then they let a boy down at the end of a rope to find out if Crotty had much food. Crotty could easily have killed the boy, but he didn't. All he had was one loaf of bread, but he promised the boy that he would save his life if he told the soldiers that Crotty had enough food to last a month. When the boy was pulled up, he told the soldiers that Crotty had no shortage of food.

'There's no use waiting any longer, if that's the case,' said the officer.

Crotty was safe for that time. When he was caught later on, he was tried and sentenced to be hanged in Waterford. He asked three times in the court-room was there anybody present from Comshingaun, but nobody answered. They were all afraid to have anything to do with him. He then said that there was a bootful of gold hidden in Comshingaun under a big rock which had the imprint of a horse's hoof on it. About sixty years ago there was a farmer in Curraheen, who was very poor. He had a boy herding on the mountain, and one day the boy went home and told him that he had seen a big rock on the mountain with a mark like a horse's hoof on it. Next morning the two of them went to the rock. The farmer sent the boy home for something, and said that he would do the herding that day. Nobody knows what happened, but the farmer didn't see a poor day from that on. He had cows and land everywhere, but the poor boy got nothing out of it.

For accounts of the life and exploits of 'Crotty the Robber', see: *J. W. & S. E. I. Arch. Socy.*, XII, 2, 80-98 ; also O'Hanlon, *The Highwayman in Irish History*, 106–112. Crotty was hanged in Waterford in 1742.

81 *Willie Brennan*

Brennan was born in Kilmurry, near Kilworth. He listed in the army and then he deserted out of it. They were hunting him around the country day and night. One day outside at Leary's Bridge, Brennan met the Pedlar Bawn. I never heard him called by any other name. The Pedlar was travelling for a firm in Cork, going about the country selling different kinds of things. Brennan put the blunderbuss up to him and made him hand out what he had, watch and chain and all. Then the Pedlar asked him to give him some token to show to the people of the firm in Cork that he had met him.

'Tell them that you met Brennan the Highwayman.'

'Give me some token that you met me, or I'll be put to jail,' said the Pedlar.

'What have I to do for you ?' asked Brennan.

'Fire a shot through this side of my old coat,' said the Pedlar. He did.

'Fire another through this side now' said the Pedlar. So he did.

'Here !' said the Pedlar. 'Fire another through my old hat !' Brennan did.

'Come !' said the Pedlar. 'Fire another through my old cravat !'

'I have no more ammunition,' said Brennan.

The Pedlar then drew a pistol, wherever he had it hid.

'Come !' said he. 'Deliver !'

Brennan had to deliver, quick and lively too !

'You're a smarter man than me,' said he. 'All I ever went through, I robbed army, men and lords, and you beat me ! Will you make a comrade for me ?'

The Pedlar only flung his pack over the ditch.

'I will,' said he. 'I'll stand a loyal comrade until my dying day.'

And so he was, a loyal comrade.

'We'll go along to County Tipperary,' said Brennan. ' 'Tis a wealthy county. There's agents and landlords there going around the country gathering the rent in the houses, and we'll whip them going back in the evening.'

So the two of them went along to the County Tipperary. Brennan went in to a widow there one morning. The poor woman was crying and lamenting. He asked her what was the matter with her.

'What good is it for me to tell you, my good man ?' said she.

She didn't know but he was a tramp.

'How do you know ?' said he.

'The agent is coming here bye-and-bye, and I haven't a halfpenny to give him for the rent,' said she.

'Well, what would you say to the man who'd give it to you ?' said Brennan.

He asked her how much it was, and she told him – five or six pounds, I suppose. He counted it out to her.

'Tell me now,' said he, 'the road he goes home in the evening.'

She told him the road he'd take after giving the day gathering around. He made her go down on her knees then and swear to God and to him that she would never tell anyone that she saw him, or mention that anyone gave her the money. Himself and the Pedlar met the agent going home with the money and whipped the whole lot that he had gathered that day.

Brennan is buried over in Kilcrumper near the old church wall.

Willie Brennan's favourite haunts for his exploits were the Kilworth area of North Cork and the adjacent districts of South Tipperary. He was active in the early nineteenth century and, like many other men of his kind, had the reputation of robbing the rich and helping the poor. A ballad, 'Brennan on the Moor', which is still sung, serves to keep his memory alive.

82 *The Scorach of Glenane*

There was a robber living in Glenane one time, and the name the people had for him was the Scorach. He lived in a kind of cave about three miles of Casla Bay. You would have to crawl into the cave, but you could stand straight up within four feet of the entrance. The cave was eight feet in height and about seven in width ; there was a cliff on every side of it, and it had a roof of rough stones covered with heather on the outside. It was as dry as a mill. That was the Scorach's house.

He was six feet five inches tall, and weighed eighteen stone. He never wore a hat or a cap. He resembled a cliff in build, wide and strong in bone and skin. Nothing was more like his two jaws than a long wide board of oak. He was a Naughton from both his father's and his mother's side. He had never planted a potato in his life, nor had he dug one ; he lived on beef and mutton, and they weren't his own either. He would often travel ten miles to steal a beef. When times were bad, he used to talk around through the townlands, enquiring if there was anybody badly off. If he heard about somebody like that, he would go off and kill a beef, and give it to those who were hungry.

He got news one day of some families who were hungry. Blake, the landlord at Tully, had a three-year-old bull that he had bought at Nephin. This bull was so big and wide that a man could sleep on his back ! The Scorach set out one morning with five other men ; they killed the bull, divided it into four quarters, and left two portions in the house where the hungry family lived. They kept the other two quarters and hid them in a bog-hole.

'Now, men,' said the Scorach, 'let ye go home. When Blake hears that his bull is missing, the first thing he'll do is to go to Claregalway for the Revenue people. I'll cross over the bog and I'll meet him on his way, so he'll never suspect that it was I who killed his bull.'

Off he went, and he never stopped until he reached Galway. He got a little mug of fresh butter-milk and a cake from a man called Big Anthony, who lived there at Fahabeg. Then he walked west along the road, until he met Séamus Blake and his wife at Caorán Mór, above Salthill.

'Oh, Lord !' said Blake, when he saw the Scorach. ' 'Tis wrong for a person to say anything. Hundreds are hung in the wrong. I was certain that this was the fellow who had taken my bull.'

The Scorach could hear him saying this to his wife. Blake turned back home and sent out his bailiffs to search for the bull, but they got no account of it or where it had gone.

The Scorach then went to steal and rob in the districts of Moycullen and Oughterard. He never stole a cow or a sheep from a poor person, but he brought them to those who were in need. He carried in his pocket a small hammer, without a handle, and with that he used to kill the animals by striking them on the forehead with it. He would then draw their blood, take the carcase on his back to Cloghernamruck and skin it. Then he would cut it into quarters and hide them in a covered hole until he heard of somebody who was badly off. Many's the person whose life he saved, who would have died of hunger but for him.

It was a man named Long Tadhg who informed on him. Tadhg lived in Derryhurk, and the Scorach stole a heifer from him. The governor of the prison thought it a pity that such a fine man should be in jail. He wrote to the Queen and the Scorach was released. He was asked would he like to join the army. He said that he would : it would be preferable to the life he was leading, being chased like a hare. He was given the choice of joining the army or the navy. He said he'd prefer the navy. He was given four days to see his people before he left, and that's when he made a song about his adventures.

The Irish word, *Scorach,* by which this folk-hero was known, means a fellow. County Galway was, so far as is known, the main scene of his exploits.

83 *James Freney*

In his young days Freney was a stable-boy for some big gentleman in County Wexford. One day a land-agent came to visit the gentleman ; he had been out gathering the rent all day and had a big bag of money with him. He stayed with the gentleman until night. Freney brought his horse around to the hall-door for the agent when he was about to take his departure. The gentleman of the house came out to the hall-door with him.

'If I were you, I wouldn't venture home tonight,' said he to the agent. ' 'Tisn't safe these times to be travelling at night with money.'

The agent only laughed at him. He produced a revolver, and says he :

'Where is the man will rob me while I have this ?'

He mounted his horse, anyway, and off he goes. Freney said to himself that he would see what the agent was made of, so he got another horse out of the stable and took a short-cut through the fields. He was at a lonely part of the road before the agent. He got an old cabbage-stump then and waited for his man. When the agent came along, Freney stepped out on the road in front of him and ordered him to hand over all he had. Faith, he did quickly ! The agent gave him his own revolver and turned back towards the gentleman's house again. Freney went back the same way again and he was in time to attend to the agent's horse when he arrived at the hall-door. As soon as the agent arrived, the gentleman came out to the hall-door.

'What's wrong ?' he asked.

'I was robbed,' said the agent.

'You had right to take my advice and stay here for the night,' said the gentleman.

'They wouldn't have robbed me,' said the agent, 'but they were too many for me. There were about fifty of them in it.'

Freney was listening to this going on and he couldn't stick it any longer, hearing all the lies the agent was spinning. So he drew the wallet out of his pocket and gave it to the agent.

'Here's your money,' says he, 'and here's what I robbed you with,' showing him the cabbage-stump.

Both the agent and the gentleman sent for the police on the spot, but Freney took to his heels and got away. That is how Freney came to be a highwayman. One day he came along to a little house on the side of a hill. He went in, and there was an old man sitting by the fire. He asked if he would let him sit by the fire for a while as the day was cold. The old man said he could, and welcome. So he sat down, and the two talked and chatted for a while. It wasn't long till Freney noticed that the old man was gloomy and depressed over something, with his head down over the fire.

'What's wrong with you, my good man?' says Freney.

'I'll tell you,' says the old man. 'The landlord is coming here tomorrow for the rent, and I haven't the money for him. I'll be thrown out.'

'Cheer up!' says Freney. 'Tell me who is the landlord.'

The old man told him. Freney then asked him how much was the rent. When the old man told him, Freney put his hand in his pocket, counted out the money, put it into an envelope and handed it to the old man.

'Take this now and go up to the landlord with it,' says Freney. 'I'll wait until you come back.'

The old man was delighted and set off, with two hearts, to the landlord's house. He went in to the landlord.

'I'm glad to say I've come to you with the rent, sir', said he.

'Where did you get it?' asked the landlord.

'A man came into the house and gave it to me,' says the old man.

'What kind of a man was he?'

The old man described him.

'Here,' says the landlord, 'take back this money! I'll forgive you the rent this time.'

The old man came back, delighted with himself.

'Well,' says Freney, 'how did you get on?'

'Oh, fine entirely! He asked me where I got the money, and I told him. Then he asked me to describe you to him, and when I did, he gave me back the money and said that he'd forgive me the rent this time.'

'You may bet he didn't take it !' says Freney. 'He knew well, if he did, that he'd lose ten times as much !'

The old man was giving him back the money then.

'Keep it, my good man,' says Freney, 'and buy things that you'll want for yourself and the children.'

Freney always had a home there after that, if he was tired or if he wanted to hide from the soldiers.

For an account of the exploits of 'Freney the Robber' in the middle of the eighteenth century, see : *The Life and Adventures of James Freney* supposedly written by himself, *JRSAI* IV (1856), 53-60 ; and O'Hanlon, *The Highwayman in Irish History,* 97-105.

84 *Paul Jones*

Some of the Murphies in Valentia Island are called the 'Paul Joneses'. This is how they got the name.

One time Tim Murphy and five other men were fishing for pollock or gurnard out in the bay, northwest of Valentia. They saw what looked like a ship far away to the west of them. She came towards them, and they began to talk to the captain. He asked them would they like to go on board to look over the ship ; all that they need do was to tie up their boat alongside. He gave them a rope to do so, and they went on board. They walked through the ship and had dinner and some drinks.

When the time came to leave, the captain said that he was short one man of his crew and he would keep Tim Murphy. Tim was a fine-looking man, the best of the six. The rest of the fishermen said that that wouldn't do at all, as his people would charge them of having murdered him, if he didn't return along with them. They would be arrested and hanged, they said. The captain said that there was a danger of that, but if they told the truth and stood by it, nothing would happen to them.

When they reached home, they told their story, but, if they did, they weren't believed. They were arrested and charged in court, but when they all had the same story to tell, without changing it, they were allowed to go free. I heard that Tim had a wife and four children. He spent eight years on Paul Jones's ship until it was wrecked on the coast of Spain. Just before that, the captain divided the spoils among his crew. Tim faced for home on some ship that brought him to Valentia. He had a big bag of money on his back. After nightfall one evening, in he came to his wife. When she saw him, she fainted, as she thought he was a ghost from the other world. When she recovered, he told her to have no fears ; he wasn't dead yet, even though he had been gone eight years.

He and his wife continued on, and he bought some farms with all the money he had. Ever after that, he was called Tim Paul, and those who came after him were called the 'Paul Joneses'.

John Paul Jones (1747-92) was an American, who raided British ships in the Atlantic in the 1770s when England was at war with her American colonies. This story may have a factual basis.

XI
Places

This final category of legends may be divided into two sections : those which tell how a place or other feature of the landscape came into being, and those which seek to explain the origin of a place-name. Both types are very common in Ireland and, indeed, in every other country also.

85 *Lough Derg*

There was no country in the world had more witchcraft than Ireland before Saint Patrick came. He spent forty days in the snow on top of Croagh Patrick praying for some means of banishing the demons from the mountain, but it was all in vain. He had no bed on which to lay his head, only the snow, and it was freezing and snowing. He prayed to Almighty God to give him some way to banish the demons from the mountain.

Then a bell fell beside him from the sky, and every time he threw the bell at them, he killed a great number. At last he had them all killed except the Caorthanach (the Devil's mother). She raced down from the mountain, and he followed her with the bell. He threw it at her at a place called Rosseecarham and knocked her down. That place is named after her to this day.

She never stopped until she reached Ulster, and he followed her. She went out into a lake there. As she was doing that, he threw his bell at her and killed her. The lake was red with her blood, and that's why it is called Lough Derg (the Red Lake) from that day to this. The lake is a holy one, and every one who goes that way makes a pilgrimage to it.

> Croagh Patrick is a mountain in County Mayo, and is still the centre of a great Catholic pilgrimage (see Legend No. 43). Lough Derg, to which thousands of Catholics go on pilgrimage each year from 1 June to 15 August, is in County Donegal, about ten miles to the east of the town of that name. For reference to the Devil's mother (*Caorthanach*) see Legend No. 13.

86 *The Seven Churches*

There was a poor man there long ago. He and his wife had a big family. He said that he would leave her for seven years. He came back after the seven years, and nine months later his wife gave birth to seven children in one 'round'. The father then said that he would drown them. He put them into a basket, and took it on his back to drown them. On the road he met a priest who asked him what he had in the basket. He said he had little pups. The priest didn't believe him and told him to let down the basket to see what was in it. When he did this, the priest saw the seven baby boys and told the father that he should be ashamed to do such a thing. The man said that he couldn't help it, he had no means of rearing them.

Then the priest baptised the first one, and said that he would keep him for himself. He baptised the others too and sent them to be reared by six priests. When the seven grew up, they all became priests. The Seven Churches in Lough Derg are named after them. They say that's a true story, any way!

The legend of the seven babies who were saved from drowning and later became bishops was popular in many parts of Ireland. There are many old ecclesiastical centres where seven churches stood in former centuries.

87 *Fair Head*

I couldn't say for sure how this story came, but I do believe it was told on the island (Rathlin) and I heard it told; but I've also heard it was seen in books. It was a Swedish or a Norwegian king who was coming to Rathlin to marry the King of Rathlin's daughter. The king lived, they say, here on that round hill you can see from our gate. The girl didn't want to marry him. They said the Swedish king was attracted by the glossy piece he had seen from the sea at Greenan; they said there was coal there, but that it wouldn't blaze, only burn with a red glow. Anyhow, there was an open-air dance, and he bribed one of the King of Rathlin's henchmen to dance the girl over the cliffs. And he did, and they both went over; the girl held tight to him. She had long, lovely, fair hair, and she was got over at Fair Head, and that's why its name was changed from Benmore to Fair Head. That's the story.

Fair Head in County Antrim and the Mizen Head in County Cork are the two parts of Ireland which are furthest apart. Rathlin Island lies off the coast of County Antrim.

88 *Aaltawheel Bridge*

There is a stone at this spot, lodged between two uprights of rock.
'Tis known as Aaltawheel Bridge. It is supposed to collapse or fall
when the only son of a McCurdy man and a McCurdy woman, and
him red-haired, walks over it.

> Similarly, there are certain castles which will, it is prophesied, fall
> down when a particular person passes by. For this, see *Dublin
> University Magazine*, XVIII (1846), 403, concerning Castle Connell in
> County Limerick, which, it is said, will fall when the wisest man in
> the world will pass by it.

89 *The Beggar's Bridge*

The Beggar's Bridge is somewhere in Tipperary. This is how it got
its name. There was a young man living near a river in a very remote,
wild place, with no house near him. A rough, cold, wet night came
around Saint Brigid's Feast, and about ten o'clock the man went out
to see was there any sign of the weather improving. It was so dark
that he couldn't see his finger. He heard a voice calling for help at
the other side of the river, so he thought that it was someone in
danger of death or drowning. There was a ford across the river
nearby, but there was a high flood on it that night. Several people
had been drowned there.

He went back to the house for a lantern and lit a candle in it. He
was barely able to struggle across the ford, and the storm was nearly
knocking him down. What did he find at the other side but a poor
man caught between two rocks, and the flood rising around him! He
lifted him up, took him on his back and carried him back to the
house. He put down a big fire and warmed the old man and gave
him hot drinks.

'Only for you, this would be my last night alive,' said the old
man.

Well, to make a long story short, the old man stayed on in the
house, and he used to go around begging every day. Sometimes he
would go and sit between the two rocks at the other side of the ford.

The young man got married, and his wife was very kind to the old man. At last he got sick and stayed in bed altogether.

' 'Tis a long time now since you saved my life', said he to the young man, 'and I must tell you who I am. I was a sailor in my young days, and many's the port and harbour I sailed into. When my health failed me, the owners of the ship told me that they had no more use for me, so all I could do was to go around begging. I often crossed over the ford here, without you seeing me. My life is nearly over now, and you must bring me the priest. When I die, you must put into the grave with me the purse that I have inside my cap, except when I'm in bed. That's all I want you to do.'

The priest came and anointed him, and it wasn't long until he died. The young man took good care to bury the purse in the coffin. On the night after the funeral, the young man had a dream in which he thought that he heard the voice of the beggar telling him to open the grave again and to take out the purse. He had the same dream the next night and the next, so his wife advised him to do what the voice told him. He went to the graveyard the following night, opened the grave, took the purse out of the coffin and brought it back to the house. When they opened it, it was full of golden guineas. They were delighted at all the riches they had got, and no wonder!

But for the next three nights, they couldn't get any sleep at all. The chairs and tables and everything else were being thrown around the house, and it was only when the cock crowed that the noise stopped. The man was sure that it was the ghost of the old man was causing the trouble, so he went to the priest and told him about it. The man wanted to put the money back into the coffin again, but the priest told him to wait for another day. The noise wasn't so bad that night. Next day, the priest said that he would give the money to the county council so that they could build a bridge across the ford, and he would ask them to put the beggar's name printed on it. When that was done, they were able to sleep soundly at night.

After that they searched between the two rocks where the beggar used to sit sometimes, and they found all the coppers that he had collected by begging. So they were able to live happily from that time out.

The Feast of Saint Brigid is on 1 February.

90 *Saint Finbar and the River Lee*

Long long ago, before Saint Finbar came to Gougane, the little lake was between the mountains, and on a calm day you would like to be looking at it, the water was so still. At that time there was a small house there and a widow and her son lived in it. They had one cow, and every day the son would mind the cow while his mother was busy around the house.

One day when he went down to the lake, what did he see, instead of the water, but an ugly serpent that was almost as big as one of the hills around! The boy was terrified and he ran home. They didn't know from where the serpent had come or why she came, so there was great excitement around the place. The serpent remained there and came out every day and swept off anything she met. At last the people of the district were ruined, and were afraid to go outside their doors.

Saint Finbar came to the district and the people begged him to do something for them. They had no great faith in the saint for the parish priest had spent his time trying to banish the serpent. That was good and it wasn't bad! One night when the great world was asleep, and the serpent along with them, Saint Finbar went out with two of his friars. He never halted until he reached the lake. He walked around it three times, praying. When he reached the mouth of the lake the third time, he stopped, took out a small bottle of holy water that he had and sprinkled it three times on the serpent. The serpent shook herself and let out a roar that shook the hills round-about. Then she moved from where she was and tore and devoured the land until she came to where Lough Loo is today. She made a bed there for herself. Next morning she moved on again and never stopped till she reached Cork Harbour. There she entered the sea.

Water has filled the track she left behind her, and that's the River Lee today. The people of the place were so grateful to Saint Finbar that they drew stones and earth and made a small island in the middle of the lake. There he built a monastery.

Saint Finbar is the patron saint of Cork, and his name is often given to male children. The River Lee rises near Ballingeary in County Cork and flows eastwards to the city where it enters Cork Harbour. Gougane is a beautiful lake, surrounded by high mountains, where there is an ancient church, dedicated to Saint Finbar ; it is a place of pilgrimage.

91 *Lake Inchiquin*

There was a man named Quin living near Corofin in the old times. He lived near where Lough Inchiquin is now. He was a gentleman and he kept race-horses. It happened that a young woman who was under a spell used to be seen coming out of the lake. The gentleman married her, but before she lived with him she said that she would not stay with him, for even a day or a night, if anyone of the O'Brien's of Killowen came to the house. These were the O'Briens whom the mermaid had cursed for having kept her a prisoner for a time.

Quin was getting on well with the race-horses. Then one day he met one of the O'Briens, whom the mermaid had cursed, and O'Brien said to him:

'Why don't you invite me to your house, and you getting on so well in the world with your horses? Wouldn't you invite me some night?'

'If that's the way, come tonight,' said Quin.

I suppose that he forgot the promise he had given to his wife. O'Brien came that night. When the woman of the house saw him, all she did was to go to the clothes-chest and unlock it. She took out her head-dress and took her two children out through the window. They went into the lake. When her husband saw this he followed them into the lake, and none of them was seen from that day to this. That's why the lake was called Lough Inchiquin, and that's its name ever since.

This legend (see Legend No. 31) is given here to explain how the lake was named after a man named Quin. The lake is situated near the village of Corofin in County Clare.

92 *The Aran Islands and Lough Corrib*

When Finn mac Cool was the leader of the Fianna of Ireland long ago, a band of plunderers used to come here from Greece or some other country under the sun. They were great robbers. At that time one of the old Irish chieftains was living where Lough Corrib is now. Galway City wasn't in existence at all then. This chieftain was very wealthy. One night the sea-robbers came, killed the old chieftain and all those who were living with him, burned the castle and stole all the fine, valuable jewels that were in it. Then they sailed away over the sea with their prizes.

Sometimes after that, Finn mac Cool was hunting in West Connacht. When he heard about what had happened,

'Bad news!' said he. 'But if they come again, I'll drive them out with my magic.'

While he was saying that, he took hold of a piece of land with his two hands, and threw it out towards the mouth of Galway Bay. It broke into four pieces. One of them fell far out into the sea, and the other three fell nearer to the dry land. That's how the Aran Islands came to be, and Lough Corrib came where he had pulled up the piece of land.

But that's not the end of the story! My father, God rest his soul, used to tell it finely. The piece of land that fell far out in the sea sank down under it when the sun set. Sometime after that, the sea-robbers came back, and when they were sailing over the sunken island, it rose up by magic and sank again, taking their ships and everything else along with it. They never rose again. But, my father used to say: 'If it rises again, may God help Galway City! It will disappear for ever.'

The Aran Islands (Inishmore, Inishmaan and Inisheer) lie off the west coast of County Galway. Lough Corrib is a large lake in the same county; its southern tip extends to the city of Galway.

93 *Aunascaul Lake*

Long ago in the time of the Fianna, there was a big giant called Cúchulainn living in a castle on the top of Dromvally mountain. The ruins of the castle are there today, and it is called Tigh Chúchulainn or Cúchulainn's House. But, as I said before, this giant was living there and he owned all this part of the country. He had an army of big giants with him, and they used to be out hunting every day. At that time this part of the country was full of big woods, and there was a lot of wild animals, such as the wild boar and very big deers, the size of a horse. There used to be big, wild bulls in the woods too.

Cúchulainn and his men used to kill a lot of them to eat them; every man could eat a boar or bull, and it would be but one meal for him. If he ate that feed in the morning, he would be hungry in the evening or in the middle of the day, the same as any man.

At that time there was a very beautiful woman living in a house by the side of Aunascaul Lake, near Dromvally. Her name was Scál Ní Mhúrnáin. Cúchulainn was very fond of her, and he used always bring her food. At that time there was a big giant living in the north of Ireland, and he heard of this nice-looking woman, so he made up his mind to come down and take her away. He started off and came to Aunascaul Lake and met Scál Ní Mhúrnáin. He told her to come away with himself and he would give her all the gold she wanted. She refused to go with him, but he said that, if she would not come of her own will, he would take her by force. He took her up in his arms and was going away with her when Cúchulainn came to the top of the cliff on the Dromvally side of the lake. When he saw the giant going away with the woman, he made a shout, and it was so loud and fierce that it shook the cliffs around and knocked some of the stones off them. When the other giant heard all the stones falling, he was full sure that he was done for. He let the woman down on the ground and ran up the side of Coomduff Hill until he came to the top of the cliff. When the woman saw herself free, she ran into her own house and shut the door.

When the giant from the north of Ireland looked across to Dromvally cliff, he saw Cúchulainn standing there and he took up a big rock and threw it at Cúchulainn, thinking that it might kill him. He missed Cúchulainn, but if he did, Cúchulainn took up another big rock and threw it at the giant. A big battle started between the two giants, throwing rocks at each other, each about a half-ton weight. The battle went on for a full week. At the end of the week, Scál Ní Mhúrnáin came out of the house and she saw all the rocks flying across the air. She stood looking at them for a long time. At last Cúchulainn stopped throwing the stones, and the giant on Coomduff cliff shouted out:

'You are done at last! I knew that I would finish you!'

When he said that, he got a fit of laughing that shook the cliff. When Scál Ní Mhúrnáin heard him saying that and laughing, she was full sure that Cúchulainn was killed and that she would be taken away by the giant. She couldn't bear that, so she got one mad fit and ran right up to the edge of the lake and threw herself in. She was drowned. At the same time, Cúchulainn was rooting a big rock out of the side of the hill. Just as he had the rock raised up over his head, he looked down at the lake, and he saw the woman, and she drowning. He knew that he had no hope of saving her. He raised the big stone over his head and threw it with all his might and power and struck the giant with it. The giant fell dead on the spot. Then Cúchulainn ran down the side of the mountain and up to the lake. There in the bottom of the lake he saw the dead body of Scál Ní Mhúrnáin, and she drowned. He started to cry at the top of his voice in lamentation after her. He told his men that they wouldn't leave her body at the bottom of the lake, so some of them went home and brought a long rope with a hook at the end of it and pulled her body out of the water. They took it up the side of Dromvally Mountain and dug a grave and buried it there. Even till today, no furze grows on that part of the mountain, and the shape of the woman can be seen for miles away by the green grass growing on top of her grave. They then went to Coomduff cliff and got the giant's body. They threw it down the cliff and piled a heap of stones on top of it; but they didn't cover it too well, and the wild animals came and ate him.

It is said that is the reason why the lake got its name of Loch an Scáil, after Scál Ní Mhúrnáin.

This lake lies in the Dingle Peninsula, about twenty miles to the southwest of Tralee. The mountain called Slieve Mish towers above it, and the ancient remains of 'Cúchulainn's House' lies on its slope. Cúchulainn was probably a god in origin, and he was the main hero of the Ulster Cycle of storytelling.

References

ABBREVIATIONS

IFC Ms. Irish Folklore Collections Manuscript (in University College, Dublin).
IFC S. Ms. Irish Folklore Collections, Schools Manuscript, same venue.
FFC Folklore Fellows Communications, Helsinki.
J.R.S.A.I. Journal of the Royal Society of Antiquaries of Ireland.
J. W. & S. E. I. Arch. Socy. Journal of the Waterford and South-east Ireland Archaeological Society.
Sc. Cráibh. Scéalta Cráibhtheacha (Religious Tales), Béaloideas (Journal of the Folklore of Ireland Society), XXI (1952).

I   FATE, pages 15-20

1   IFC Ms. Vol. 171 : 422-3. Recorded in Irish by Liam Mac Meanman, full-time collector, 22 January 1936, from Paidí Tiomanaidhe (25), Golladubh, Parish of Donegal, County Donegal.
2   IFC Ms. Vol. 967 : 234-5. Recorded in Irish by Seosamh Ó Dálaigh, full-time collector, 7 January 1945, from Seán Ó Criothain (67), Kilmaelkedar, Dingle Peninsula, County Kerry.
3   IFC Ms. Vol. 158 : 12-18. Recorded in Irish by Ediphone, by Liam Mac Coisdeala, full-time collector, 8 November 1935, from Pádhraic Mac an Iomaire, Coillín, Carna, County Galway.
4   IFC Ms. Vol. 1474 : 30-1. Recorded in Irish by Tadhg Ó Murchú, full-time collector, 15 February 1956, from Domhnall Ó Murchú, Imleach Mór, Ballinskelligs, County Kerry.

II THE DEVIL, pages 21-35

5 IFC Ms. Vol. 244 : 254-7 (*Sc. Cráibh*. No. 51, 102-3). Recorded in Irish by Seosamh Ó Dálaigh, full-time collector, 28 September 1936, from Seán Ó Grífín (58), Cathair Boilg, Parish of Ventry, County Kerry.

6 IFC Ms. Vol. 472 : 53-60 (*Sc. Cráibh*. No. 40, 99-102). Recorded in Irish by Seán Ó Heochaidh, full-time collector, from Conall Mac Cormaic (75), Doire Leac Conaill, Parish of Templecrone, County Donegal.

7 IFC Ms. Vol. 1129 : 119-121. (*Béaloideas* XI (1941), 29-30). Recorded in Irish by An tAthair Donncha Ó Floinn in the 1930s from Conchobhar Ó Síocháin of Cape Clear Island, County Cork.

8 IFC Ms. Vol. 261 : 51-4 (*Sc. Cráibh*. No. 39, 98-9). Recorded in Irish by Aodh Ó Domhnaill, 12 July 1936, from Seán Mac Grianna (32), Rann na Feirste, Parish of Templecrone, County Donegal.

9 IFC Ms. Vol. 404 : 413-20. Recorded in English by Seán Ó Flannagáin, full-time collector, in 1937, from Séamus Ó Ceallaigh, Killeen, Parish of Kiltartan, County Galway.

10 IFC Ms. Vol. 78 : 111-4. Recorded in Irish by Cáit Ní Mhainnín, October 1933, from Bríd, Bean Shéamuis de Búrca, Inbhear, Rosmuc, County Galway.

11 *Béaloideas* III (1932), 8-9. Recorded in Irish by An Seabhac (Pádraig Ó Siochfhrú) in 1930 from Pats Mhaurice Ó Grífín (75), Baile Reo, Dingle Peninsula, County Kerry.

12 IFC Ms. Vol 744 : 270-1. Recorded in English by Patrick J. O'Sullivan, 14 February 1941, from Michael O'Sullivan (76), Derrygorman, Aunascaul, County Kerry.

III ORIGINS, pages 37-51

13 IFC Ms. Vol. 277 : 261-4 (*Sc. Cráibh*. No. 92, 208-9). Recorded in Irish by Pádhraic Bairéad, 16 January, 1937, from Seán Ó Maoilfheabhail (69), Deibhleán, Parish of Kilmore, County Mayo.

14 IFC Ms. Vol. 42 : 297-300 (*Sc. Cráibh*. No. 77, 190-1). Recorded in Irish by Áine Ní Chróinín, 15 August, 1932, from Diarmaid Mac Coitir, Doire na Sagart, Ballyvourney, County Cork.

15 IFC Ms. Vol. 54 : 369. Recorded in English by Tomás Ó Ciardha, July, 1934, from Michael Donegan (65), Araglin, Parish of Kilworth, County Cork.

16 IFC Ms. Vol. 1010 : 144-5. Recorded in Irish by Liam Mac Coisdeala, May 1946, by Ediphone, from Mícheál Ó Coileáin, Carnmore, Claregalway, County Galway.

17 IFC Ms. Vol. 236 : 202-3 (Sc. Cráibh. No. 3, 7). Recorded in Irish by Brian Mac Lochlainn, full-time collector, 7 May 1936, from Bean Uí Allmhúráin (86), Cluain idir dhá Abhainn, Parish of Kill, County Galway.

18 IFC Ms. Vol. 182 : 555-6 (Sc. Cráibh. No. 10, 13-14). Recorded in Irish by Liam Mac Coisdeala, 26 May, 1936, from Seán de Búrc (80), Áth Chloigín, Parish of Anach Cuain, County Galway.

19 IFC Ms. Vol. 1129 : 101-2. Recorded in Irish by An tAthair Donncha Ó Floinn in the 1930s from Conchobhar Ó Síocháin, Cape Clear Island, County Cork.

20 IFC Ms. Vol. 969 : 384-6 (Sc. Cráibh. No. 59, 164-5). Recorded in Irish by Calum Mac Gilleathain, 11 January 1945, from Maitiú Mór Ó Tuathail, Indreabhán, County Galway.

21 IFC Ms. Vol. 409 : 47-50 (Sc. Cráibh. No. 62, 168-9). Recorded in Irish by Áine Nic an Liagha, 27 July 1937, from Cáit, Bean Uí Ghallchobhair (90), An Ráth Íocht., Parish of Cloghaneelly, County Donegal.

22 IFC Ms. Vol. 1176 : 64-5. Recorded in English by Philip J. Gaynor, 20 October 1949, from James Argue (86), Galbolia, Kingscourt, County Cavan.

23 IFC Ms. Vol. 195 : 375-8 (Sc. Cráibh. No. 134, 277-8). Recorded in Irish by Anraoi Ó Corrdhuibh, 1936, from Seán Ó Roithleáin (70), Ros Dumhach, Parish of Achú, County Mayo.

24 IFC S. Ms. Vol 426 : 214-5. Recorded in Irish by a school-child, 1937, from Mícheál Ó Brosnacháin, Minard West, Lispole, County Kerry.

25 IFC Ms. Vol. 143 : 2306-8 (Sc. Cráibh. No. 8, 12-13). Recorded in Irish by Seán Ó Heochaidh, full-time collector, 19 February 1936, from Pádhraic Mac Fhionnlaoich (80), Mín an Chearbhaigh, Parish of Glencolmkille, County Donegal.

26 IFC Ms. Vol. 1127 : 117 (Béaloideas XI (1941), 28). Recorded in Irish in the 1930s by An tAthair Donncha Ó Floinn from Conchobhar Ó Síocháin, Cape Clear Island, County Cork.

27 IFC Ms. Vol. 1159 : 62. Recorded in English by Michael J. Murphy, full-time collector, 27 July 1948, from Francis Quinn, Farsnagh, Coagh, County Tyrone.

IV   THE SUPERNATURAL, pages 53-78

28 IFC Ms. Vol. 181 : 434-7. Recorded on an Ediphone in Irish by Liam Mac Coisdeala, full-time collector, 7 April 1936, from Seán a Búrca (80), Áth Chloigín, Parish of Anach Cuain, County Galway.
29 IFC Ms. Vol. 937 : 328-30. Recorded in Irish by Seán Ó Cróinín, full-time collector, December, 1943, from Amhlaoimh Ó Loingsigh, Cúil Ao, County Cork.
30 IFC Ms. Vol. 158 : 171-3. Recorded in Irish by Liam Mac Coisdeala, full-time collector, 22 November 1935, from Pádhraic Mac an Iomaire, Coillín, Carna, County Galway.
31 IFC Ms. Vol. 55 : 260-6. Recorded in Irish by Brian Mac Cathbhaid, 1931, from Johnny Sheimisín Ó Domhnaill (74), Rann na Feirste, County Donegal.
32 IFC Ms. Vol. 31 : 113-5. Recorded in Irish on an Ediphone by Seán Ó Súilleabháin, 3 August 1933, from Mort Ó Sé, school-teacher, Adrigole, County Cork.
33 IFC Ms. Vol. 203 : 398-404. Recorded in Irish by Pádraig Ó Conaill, 1916, from Cáit Nic Aonghusa (79), Bréantráigh, West Carbery, County Cork.
34 IFC Ms. Vol. 430 : 109-115. Recorded in Irish on an Ediphone by Seosamh Ó Dálaigh, full-time collector, 14 September 1937, from Seán Ó Grífín (60), Cathair Boilg, Parish of Ventry, County Kerry. He had heard the story fifty years previously from Siobhán Ní Shúilleabháin (50), of the same district.
35 IFC Ms. Vol. 529 : 216-220. Recorded on an Ediphone in Irish by Liam Mac Coisdeala, full-time collector, 22 September 1938, from Éamon a Búrc (72), Áill na Brón, Kilkerrin, County Galway.
36 IFC Ms. Vol. 31 : 58-59. Recorded in Irish by Seán Ó Súilleabháin, 14 July 1933, from Domhnall Ó Dubhda, Ballyferriter, County Kerry.
37 IFC Ms. Vol. 159 : 241-5 (*Sc. Cráibh.* No. 97, 215-6). Recorded in Irish, January 1936, by Liam Mac Coisdeala, full-time collector, from Mícheál Mór Mac Donnchú (60), An Más, Carna, County Galway.

38 IFC S. Ms. Vol 426 : 213-4. Recorded in Irish by a schoolchild, 1937, from Mícheál Ó Brosnacháin (55), Minard West, Lispole, County Kerry.

39 IFC Ms. Vol. 157 : 632-6. Recorded in Irish by Liam Mac Coisdeala, full-time collector, 8 November 1935, from Pádhraic Mac an Iomaire, Coillín, Carna, County Galway. He had heard the story from his grandfather forty years previously.

40 IFC Ms. Vol. 529 : 248-51. Recorded in Irish on an Ediphone by Liam Mac Coisdeala, full-time collector, 23 September 1938, from Pádhraic Ó Cualáin (26), Áill na Brón, Kilkerrin, County Galway. He had heard the story shortly before from a woman from Bunahowna, Cloch na Rón, County Galway.

41 IFC Ms. Vol. 157 : 171-6. Recorded in Irish by Liam Mac Coisdeala, full-time collector, August 1935, from Marcus Ó Neachtain (29), Aird Mhór, Carna, County Galway. Marcus heard the story from his father, who, in turn, had heard it from his father fifty years previously.

42 IFC S. Ms. Vol. 426 : 209-10. Recorded in English by a schoolchild, 1938, from Máire, Bean Mhic Ghearailt (56), Bánóg, Parish of Minard, Aunascaul, County Kerry.

43 IFC Ms. Vol. 1476 : 265-70. Recorded in Irish by Ciarán Bairéad, full-time collector, 1956, from Mícheál Ó Síoda An Pháire Gharbh, Turloch Mór, County Galway.

V SPECIAL POWERS, pages 79-89

44 IFC. Ms Vol. 30 : 285-90. *Béaloideas* X(1940), 120-22. Recorded in Irish by Seán Ó Súilleabháin, January 1935, from Mícheál Ó Súilleabháin, Doire an Locha, Parish of Tuosist, County Kerry.

45 IFC Ms. Vol. 1052 : 414-5. Recorded in Irish by Tadhg Ó Murchú, full-time collector, 23 May 1948, from Seán (Mhártain) Ó Súilleabháin, Imleach Mór, Parish of Prior, County Kerry.

46 IFC Ms. Vol. 403 : 69-72. Recorded in Irish by Liam Mac Coisdeala, full-time collector, 11 September 1937, from Éamon a Búrc, Áill na Brón, Kilkerrin, County Galway, who had heard the story fifty-five years previously from his grandfather (75).

47 IFC Ms. Vol. 529 : 221-3. Recorded in Irish by Liam Mac Coisdeala, full-time collector, 22 September 1938, from Val Ó Donnchú (36), Bántrach Ard, Carna, County Galway.

48 *Béaloideas* V (1935), 132-3. Recorded in Irish in July-August, 1933, by An tAthair Donncha Ó Floinn, from Conchobhar Ó Síocháin (67), Cape Clear Island, County Cork.

49 IFC Ms. Vol. 1010 : 115-8. Recorded in Irish on an Ediphone by Liam Mac Coisdeala, full-time collector, May 1946, from Mícheál Ó Coileáin (70), Carn Mór, County Galway.

50 IFC Ms. Vol. 1010 : 119-121. Recorded in Irish by Liam Mac Coisdeala, full-time collector, 26 August 1946, from Mícheál Ó Coileáin (70), Carn Mór, County Galway.

51 IFC Ms. Vol. 308 : 231-2. Recorded in Irish by Tadhg Ó Murchú, full-time collector, 17 November, 1936, from Séamus Ó Héalaithe, Caherciveen, County Kerry.

52 IFC Ms. Vol. 84 : 15-17. Recorded in Irish by Seán Ó Dúnaí, 1894, from Déaglán Shéimín (65), An Currach, Ardmore, County Waterford.

VI RELIGIOUS LEGENDS, pages 91-116

53 IFC Ms. Vol. 540 : 374-8 (*Sc. Cráibh.* No. 98, 217-9). Recorded in Irish by Seán Ó Heochaidh, full-time collector, 10 October 1938, from Anna Nic Dhuibhir (55), An Loinneach, Parish of Gweedore, County Donegal.

54 IFC Ms. Vol. 191 : 476-80 (*Sc. Cráibh.* No. 104, 227-9). Recorded in Irish by Pádhraic Bairéad, 8 May, 1936, from Seán Ó Maoilfheabhail (68), Deibhleán, Parish of Kilmore, County Mayo.

55 IFC Ms. Vol. 305 : 569-73 (*Sc. Cráibh.* No. 113, 245-6). Recorded in Irish by Liam Mac Coisdeala, full-time collector, 25 January, 1937, from Máirtín Mac Cualáin (73), Loch Con Uidhre, Parish of Carna, County Galway.

56 IFC Ms. Vol. 305 : 57-8 (*Sc. Cráibh.* No. 116, 249). Recorded in Irish by Liam Mac Coisdeala, full-time collector, 21 November, 1936, from Máirtín Mac Oralaigh (74), An Mhainistir, Parish of Abbeyknockmoy, County Galway.

57 IFC Ms. Vol. 26 : 147-50 (*Sc. Cráibh.* No. 100, 222-4). Recorded in Irish by Tadhg Ó Murchú, full-time collector, 1911, from his father, An Sceachachán, Parish of Caherdaniel, County Kerry.

58 IFC Ms. Vol. 236: 480-1 (*Sc. Cráibh.* No. 95, 214-5). Recorded in Irish by Brian Mac Lochlainn, full-time collector, 18 July 1936, from Máirtín Seoighe (51), Doire Bhéil an Mháma, Parish of Muighros, County Galway.

59 IFC Ms. Vol. 308 : 58-63 (*Sc. Cráibh*. No. 101, 224-5). Recorded in Irish by Tadhg Ó Murchú, full-time collector, 1 March 1936, from Pádraig Mac Gearailt (77), Cill an Ghoirtín, Parish of Dromad, County Kerry.

60 IFC Ms. Vol. 143 : 1762-5 (*Sc. Cráibh*. No. 112, 244-5). Recorded in Irish by Seán Ó Heochaidh, full-time collector, 4 January, 1936, from Seán Mac Fhionnlaoich (90), Malin, Parish of Glencolmkille, County Donegal.

61 IFC Ms. Vol. 1035 : 152-6 (*Sc. Cráibh*. No. 105, 231-3). Recorded in Irish by Seosamh Ó Dálaigh, full-time collector, December 1947, from Muiris Ó Conchobhair (77), Baile Í Bhoithín, Parish of Marhan, County Kerry.

62 IFC Ms. Vol. 539 : 99-101 (*Sc. Cráibh*. No. 21, 26-7). Recorded in Irish by Seán Ó Heochaidh, 14 June 1938, from Seosamh Ó Colla (65), An Loinneach, Parish of Gweedore, County Donegal.

63 IFC Ms. Vol. 158 : 121-8 (*Sc. Cráibh*. No. 88, 199-202). Recorded in Irish by Liam Mac Coisdeala, full-time collector, 15 November 1935, from Pádhraic Mac an Iomaire (64), Coillín, Carna, County Galway.

64 IFC. Ms. Vol. 529 : 449-52. Recorded in Irish by Liam Mac Coisdeala, 12 October 1938, from Éamon a Búrc (72), Áill na Brón, Kilkerrin, County Galway. He had heard the story from the man to whom the event had happened sixty years previously.

65 IFC Ms. Vol. 158 : 129-34 (*Sc. Cráibh*. No. 65, 174-6). Recorded in Irish by Liam Mac Coisdeala, full-time collector, 15 November 1935, from Pádhraic Mac an Iomaire (64), Coillín, Carna, County Galway.

66 IFC Ms. Vol. 2 : 40-1 (*Sc. Cráibh*. No. 75, 188-9). Recorded in Irish by Seán Ó Dubhda, 1931, from Pádraig Ó Conchobhair, Cill Chúile, Parish of Kilmaelkedar, County Kerry.

67 IFC Ms. Vol. 354 : 294-6 (*Sc. Cráibh*. No. 73, 183-4). Recorded in Irish by Seán Ó Flannagáin, full-time collector, May 1937, from Séamus Ó Riagáin (83), Tón Raithní, Parish of Behy, County Galway.

68(a) IFC Ms. Vol. 277 : 175-7 (*Sc. Cráibh*. No. 89, 202-3). Recorded in Irish by a school-child, 1936, in Inishkea Island, County Mayo.

68(b) IFC Ms. Vol. 134 : 62-66 (*Sc. Cráibh.* No. 90, 203-5). Recorded in Irish by Pádhraic Bairéad, 10 January 1936, from Seán Ó Maoilfheabhail (60), Mullach Rua, Parish of Kilmore, County Mayo.

VII INDIVIDUAL PERSONS, pages 117-133

69 IFC Ms. Vol. 1010: 85-6. Recorded in Irish by Liam Mac Coisdeala, full-time collector, 22 August 1946, from Mícheál Ó Coileáin (70), Carn Mór, Claregalway, County Galway.
70 *Béaloideas* X (1940), 204-6. Recorded in Irish by Seán Mac Thorcail, Lough Carra area, County Mayo.
71(a) IFC Ms. Vol. 229 : 219-20. Recorded in Irish by Brian Mac Lochlainn, full-time collector, 1936, from Máiréad Ní Chonaola, Damhros Mór, Parish of Ballinakill, County Galway.
71(b) IFC Ms. Vol. 157 : 129-30. Recorded in Irish by Liam Mac Coisdeala, full-time collector, 2 September 1935, from Éamon a Búrc, Áill na Brón, Kilkerrin, County Galway.
72 IFC Ms. Vol. 1470 : 131. Recorded by Michael J. Murphy, full-time collector, June 1956, from Tommy Kinley, Caralaverty, Armoy, County Antrim.
73 *Éigse* II (1940), 28. Recorded in English by Seosamh Ó Dálaigh, full-time collector, 1940, from Mrs. Lane (80), Finuge, Lixnaw, County Kerry.
74 IFC Ms. Vol. 179: 293-5. Recorded on an Ediphone in Irish, by Seán Ó Heochaidh, full-time collector, 6 April 1936, from Mícheál Ó Haoine (23), Ceann na Coille, Parish of Glencolmkille, County Donegal.
75 IFC Ms. Vol. 407 : 251-3. Recorded in English by Peader Mac Domhnaill, 22 October 1937 from Matthew Flood (51), Kilbeg, Toem, Cappawhite, County Tipperary.
76(a) IFC Ms. Vol. 404 : 484-93. Recorded in English by Seán Ó Flannagáin, full-time collector, 21 September, 1937, from Peter Harte (66), Ínse Bhuí, Parish of Kilbekanty, County Galway.
76(b) IFC Ms. Vol. 1475: 331-5. Recorded in Irish by Tadhg Ó Murchú, full-time collector, 24 February 1957, from Domhnall Ó Murchú, Imleach Mór, Parish of Prior, County Kerry.
77 IFC Ms. Vol. 306: 485-6. Recorded in English by Conchobhar

Ó Ruairc, 30 November 1936, from D. Ó Súilleabháin (68), Gort Luachrach, Bantry, County Cork.

78 *Béaloideas* V (1935), 43. Recorded in Irish by Nioclás Breathnach, 1935, from local tradition in the Parish of Ring, County Waterford.

VII ROBBERS AND PIRATES, pages 135-146

79 IFC Ms. Vol. 9 : 249-55. Recorded in Irish by An Bráthair P. T. Ó Riain, 13 October 1932, from Seán Ó Muircheartaigh, Muiríoch, Dingle Peninsula, County Kerry.
80 IFC Ms. Vol. 87 : 129-30. Recorded in Irish by Tomás Ó Faoláin, 1932, from Pádraig Ó Milléa, Tuar an Fhíona, County Waterford.
81 IFC Ms. Vol. 54 : 323-6. Recorded in English by Tomás Ó Ciardha, 1 June 1934, from Thomas O'Riordan (78), Araglin, Kilworth, County Cork.
82 *Peadar Chois Fhairrge* (1937), 88-91, traditions recorded in Irish by Seán Mac Giollarnáth, from Peadar Mac Thuathaláin (1865-1930), Cois Fhairrge, County Galway.
83 IFC Ms. Vol. 54 : 124-9. Recorded in English by Tomás Ó Ciardha, 1935, from Mrs R. Walsh, Woodgraigue, Duncormick, County Wexford.
84 IFC Ms. Vol. 1051 : 162-6. Recorded in Irish by Tadhg Ó Murchú, full-time collector, from Mícheál Ó Siochfhrú (79), Clochán na n-Ua, Parish of Prior, County Kerry.

IX PLACES, pages 147-159

85 *Béaloideas* VIII (1930), 222-3. Recorded in Irish by Pádhraic Ó Moghráin from Tomás Mac Aodháin (85), An Pháirc Úr, Tír an Áir, County Mayo.
86 IFC Ms. Vol. 238 : 184-5. Recorded in Irish by Liam Mac Coisdeala, full-time collector, 14 August 1936, from Pádhraic Ó Huigín (76), Cill Bheidhin, Claremorris, County Mayo.
87 IFC Ms. Vol. 1365 : 172. Recorded in English by Michael J. Murphy, full-time collector, August, 1954, from Mickey Joe Anderson, Ballygeel, Rathlin Island, County Antrim.

88 IFC Ms. Vol. 1390 : 27. Recorded in English by Michael J. Murphy, full-time collector, July, 1955, from Donal McCurdy, Rathlin Island, County Antrim.

89 IFC Ms. Vol. 1476 : 270-82. Recorded by Ciarán Bairéad, full-time collector, 15 November 1956, from Mícheál Ó Síoda, An Pháirc Gharbh, Turloughmore, County Galway.

90 IFC Ms. Vol. 452 : 275-8. Recorded in Irish by Nóra Ní Chróinín, 1937, from Donncha Ó Cróinín (56), Ínse Bheag, Ballingeary, County Cork.

91 IFC Ms. Vol. 40 : 140-1. Recorded in Irish by Seán Mac Mathúna, from Pádraig Mac an Charraige (80), Cnoc an Scáth, Cill a' Seana, County Clare.

92 IFC Ms. 90 : 103-6. Recorded in Irish by Michael Price, March, 1933, from Mícheál Ó Flatharta, Aran Islands, County Galway.

93 IFC Ms. Vol. 813 : 314-22. Recorded by P. J. O'Sullivan, 1942, from Michael O'Sullivan (78), Derrygorman, Aunascaul, County Kerry.

Select Bibliography

Arv : Journal of Scandinavian Folklore, I (1945–).

Béaloideas : Journal of the Folklore of Ireland Society I (1927–).

J. Bolte & G. Polivka, *Anmerkungen zu den Kinder- und Hausmärchen der Brüder Grimm,* I-V, 1913-31

William Carleton, *Redmond Count O'Hanlon : the Irish Rapparee,* 1860

Reidar Th. Christiansen, 'The Migratory Legends' (*FFC.* No. 175), 1958

Tom Peete Cross, *Motif-Index of Early Irish Literature,* 1952

Oskar Dähnhardt, *Natursagen,* I-IV, 1909-1912

Linda Dégh, 'Folk Narrative', *Folklore and Folklife : an Introduction,* ed. Richard M. Dorson, 72-80, 1972

Dublin University Magazine, I (1833–)

Éigse : A Journal of Irish Studies, I (1939–)

James Frazer, *Folklore in the Old Testament,* I – III, (1919)

James Freney, *The Life and Adventures of James Freney* (a chapbook), c. 1750

Fritz Harkort (and Karel Peeters and Robert Wildhaber) ed. *Volksüberlieferung,* 1968

J. A. Herbert, *A Catalogue of Romances in the Department of Manuscripts in the British Museum,* 1910

Douglas Hyde, *Beside the Fire,* 1890

Legends of Saints and Sinners, 1915

Journal of the Royal Society of Antiquaries of Ireland I (1849–)

Journal of the Waterford and South-east Ireland Archaeological Society, I (1894–)

G. Kittredge, *Witchcraft in Old and New England,* 1929

Bengt av Klintberg, *Svenska Folksägner,* 1972

Lochlann, A Review of Celtic Studies, I (1958–)

Louth Archaeological Journal, I (1904–)

R. A. S. Macalister, ed. *Lebor Gabala Érenn,* I-V (1938–)

Seán Mac Giollarnáth, *Peadar Chois Fhairrge,* 1937
Máire MacNeill, *The Festival of Lughnasa,* 1962
John A. McCulloch, *The Mythology of All Races,* 1930
Terence O'Hanlon, *The Highwayman in Irish History,* 1932
Seán O Súilleabháin, ed. *Scéalta Cráibhtheacha (Béaloideas,* XXI), 1952
    Folktales of Ireland, 1966
Karel Peeters (see Fritz Harkort)
G. Polivka (see J. Bolte)
Edson Richmond, ed. *Studies in Folklore,* 1957
Isaiah Schachar, *The Judensar: a Medieval Anti-Jewish Motif and its
    History,* 1974
Dag Strömbäck, *Folklore och Filologi,* 1970
Studia Fennica I (1933–)
C. W. von Sydow, 'Niebelungendiktningen och sägnen om an
    bheoir lochlannach', *Studia germanica tillägnade E. A. Kock,* 1934
Joseph Szovérffy, *Irisches Erzählgut im Abendland,* 1957
Stith Thompson, *Motif-Index of Folk Literature,* 1966
    The Types of the Folktale, 1961
John E. Wells, *A Manual of Writings in Middle English* (1050-1400),
    1916 ff
Robert Wildhaber, see Fritz Harkort
W. G. Wood-Martin, *Traces of the Elder Faiths of Ireland,* I-II, 1902

Motif Index

These numbers are from Stith Thompson, *Motif-Index of Folk Literature*, 1966

General Index